THE STREETWISE INVESTOR

Investors the world over are worried and they have a right to be worried. Stock markets are falling everywhere, interest rates are at all-time lows and millions of ordinary people who have money in building societies, unit trusts, endowments and pensions are feeling the pinch like never before.

The time is right for **The Streetwise Investor**; the true story of the ups and downs and thrills and spills of a rare breed, a successful British stock market speculator, **Alan Moore**, who started in the 1980s. Alongside son **James Moore,** the authors have spent their investing lives moving opportunistically from one 'sure thing' to the next. This includes making a fortune in privatisation issues, exploiting the dot.com boom and quickly moving into Contracts for Difference, the new derivative that allows private investors to make the same moves as the institutional players. So, what on earth is their secret and how can ordinary investors learn and profit from their success?

The Streetwise Investor demystifies investment, explains the jargon and shows how to become an expert at assessing risk. By following the authors' volatile portfolio as prices yo-yo and learning from the case studies of their major investments (such as Eidos, Carphone Warehouse and Telewest), any investor can learn how to apply their phenomenally successful investment approach. **The Streetwise Investor** gives you the confidence in your own ability to make sensible, profitable decisions in even the most explosive market conditions.

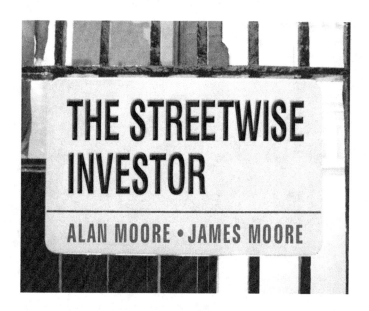

THE STREETWISE INVESTOR

ALAN MOORE • JAMES MOORE

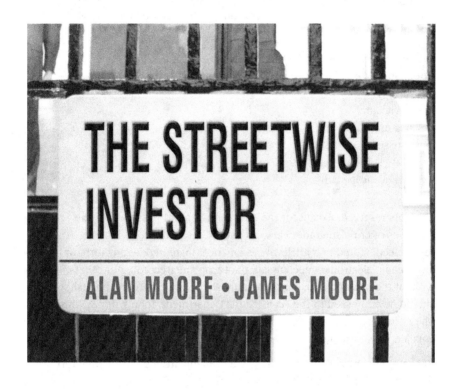

THE STREETWISE INVESTOR

ALAN MOORE • JAMES MOORE

EXTRAORDINARY INVESTING
FOR **ORDINARY** PEOPLE

CAPSTONE

First published 2004 by
Capstone Publishing Ltd (a Wiley Company)
The Atrium
Southern Gate
Chichester
West Sussex PO19 8SQ
England
www.wileyeurope.com

CIP catalogue records for this book are available from the British Library and the US Library of Congress

ISBN 1-84112-522-9

Typeset by Forewords, 109 Oxford Road, Cowley, Oxford

10 9 8 7 6 5 4 3 2

This book is printed on acid-free paper responsibly manufactured from sustainable forestry in which at least two trees are planted for each one used for paper production.

Substantial discounts on bulk quantities of Capstone Books are available to corporations, professional associations and other organizations. For details contact John Wiley & Sons: tel. (+44) 1243 770441, fax (+44) 1243 770517, email corporatedevelopment@wiley.co.uk

Contents

Acknowledgements

The authors and publishers wish to thank the following for permission to use copyright material:

Bigcharts.com for Fig. 4.1, "Techmark" from Big Charts.com, 10 April 2003; Fig. 10.1, "Eidos adjusted for 5 for 1 scrip issue", from *Big Charts.com*, 17 January 2003; Fig. 11.1, "Carphone Warehouse 2000–2003", from *Big Charts.com*, 17 January 2003; Fig. 12.1, "Telewest Communications 1996–2002", from *Big Charts.com*, 17 January 2003; Fig. 13.1, "Safeway 2000–2003", from *Big Charts.com*, 18 February 2003; Fig. 14.1, "New Look share price 1999–2002", from *Big Charts.com*, 22 January 2003.

Guardian Newspapers Ltd. for Alan Moore, "The Third Eye" from the *Guardian*, 1993.

Financial Times Ltd. for "Investors warned to shelter from 'dot bombs'", from *The Financial Times*, 3 February 2000, © 2000, Financial Times Ltd.; "Tech stocks in turmoil", from *The Financial Times*, 23 December 2000, © 2000, Financial Times Ltd.; "Lex: Hennes & Mauritz", from *The Financial Times*, 23 March 2002, © 2002, Financial Times Ltd.; "Tomb Raider helps Eidos advance", from *The Financial Times*, 20 January 1999, © 1999, Financial Times Ltd.; "Edios boosted by Lara Croft", from *The Financial Times*, 26 February 1999, © 1999, Financial Times Ltd.; "Games popularity buoys Eidos", from *The Financial Times*, 28 May 1999, © 1999, Financial Times Ltd.; "Lara Croft turns respectable and wins City friends", from *The Financial Times*, 16 December 1999, © 1999, Financial Times Ltd.; "Eidos shares fall by a third after profits warning", from *The Financial Times*, 19 January 2000, © 2000, Financial Times Ltd.; "Lex: Carphone Warehouse", from www.ft.com, 8 June 2000, © 2000, Financial Times Ltd.; "Carphone Warehouse IPO will value group at $2.4bn", from www.ft.com, 26 June 2000, © 2000, Financial Times Ltd.; "Carphone Warehouse maiden results show strong growth", from

Introduction

Somewhere back around the mid-eighties I had my very own Theory of Everything. And it worked. It was founded on two basic, seemingly incontrovertible propositions, namely (a) that I was the centre of the universe and everyone and everything else, including life itself, revolved around me, and (b) I was always right. About everything.

Simple. So simple. I wondered why no-one else had thought of it. It made life so easy. I knew for certain who I was (a Very Important Person), what I was (superior), and what everyone else was (inferior). I had an opinion on everything and as I was always right I had no need to listen to anyone else. I talked. People listened. I talked a lot. Loudly. I liked the sound of my own voice. I preached a gospel for modern living, an Epistle for the eighties.

"Wake up!" I would shout, "You're only here once. This isn't a fucking rehearsal. This is it. The real thing. And you have a decision to make – is life going to rule you or are you going to rule it? And if you want to live a life worth the living, there is only one answer to that – you have got to grab life by the balls, as hard as you can, and make it dance to your tune. Make it happen for you."

Make what happen?

"Make it big, of course! What else? It's a big world out there and it's all there for the taking. Big money! Big job! Big house! Big car! Big tits! The things we all want to get our hands on."

My credo. My litany of having. My ultimate Theory of Everything. And it had worked for me. Well, hadn't it?

I thought so on the morning of 28 June 1987 when after a bitter takeover battle I walked into the boardroom of Burns-Anderson plc and sat down at the place reserved for the Chief Executive.

At the far end of the table was Sir John Harvey-Jones, recently retired as Chairman of ICI. On my left was Roy Richardson, on my right, Don Richardson – two of the country's richest men.

The atmosphere was electric. We had won. I had won. In seven years I had gone from a desk and a filing cabinet in a Dockside warehouse to Chief Executive of a £50 million company and a £4 million personal fortune. And I was still in my thirties.

I had started from nothing. With nothing. Now I had it all. I was a hero of the Thatcherite era. In fact, I was more than self-made. I was self-created, I had cast off my beginnings and re-invented myself. And now nothing could touch me. I had gone clear.

Or so I thought…

Chapter 1

The shareholder revolution

This book is about how to make money by speculating on the stock market using some innovative tools. It's also about my personal journey as a businessman and an investor, and how my investment knowledge and skills have evolved since the heady days of the 1980s when I was a brash whiz-kid who thought he knew it all. I made a lot of money early, lost quite a bit of it, and made a lot more afterwards. I don't believe my success has merely been due to luck – I have learned how to read companies and markets, and how to adapt to the changing fashions in the City of London. My methods involve a lot of instinct and self-confidence but anyone can learn them and put them into practice. You just have to trust yourself. In this book I hope to show you how you can train yourself to become a successful speculator. I'll give you the tools, show you how they work and go through real life examples of companies I made a bundle out of. After that, it's up to you!

First, I'd like to take you back to the 1980s when the new capitalism first began. It was a great time for me because I was in the middle of it and making money. I thought I knew it all then but as I was to discover, I was only beginning my journey.

It was April 1987 and I was having a drink in a winebar in the City of London with some stock market cronies. "You could float a brick in a cardboard box and people would buy it," someone said. We all laughed. Margaret Thatcher's shareholder revolution was in full swing. With so many people getting rich fast, there was a new ethos: barrow boy chic, epitomized by the comic Harry Enfield's 'Loadsamoney' character. For the first time in generations, it was good to be greedy in Britain.

The government told us so. Share privatizations were priced to ensure that prices went up. You couldn't lose. It was almost your civic duty to be greedy. America thought so too. In New York the legendary arbitrageur Ivan Boesky even wrote a book called *Greed is Good*, which purported to explain his uncanny ability to buy shares in companies just before they came under attack by a hostile bidder, driving the share price up. What we didn't know then was that Boesky was cheating by bribing insiders for early news of takeover bids.

Would we have cared if we had known? I doubt it. We were too busy applying for shares as Margaret Thatcher sold off state-owned corporations on the stock market. There was a limit on how many one person could order on their own account, but there was a way around that – you could persuade other people to apply for shares too. My wife and my children applied, and anyone else I could find who didn't have the money or inclination to do it for themselves.

I was the Chief Executive Officer of a successful firm, so I approached my staff. Many of them were only too happy to help in return for a 10% cut of the profits. It was cheaper than giving them a Christmas bonus. By getting them to sign powers of attorney, I didn't even have to trust them to hand me my profits when the shares were sold. They wouldn't all do it, of course, but the smart ones did, the ones that could spot a good career move when they saw one.

I didn't think it was unfair. It wasn't costing them anything, since I was putting up the money and taking the risk that the share price might not rise. Not that there was any risk of that. I wouldn't have been doing it if there had been. The only way for privatization shares was up, that was the beauty of it. The government got rid of its companies, the City got rich and millions of ordinary people around the country were laughing all the way to the bank.

That's how it was. The government's policy of popular capitalism was a huge success. We all became share owners, but only for as long as it took to get on the phone and sell them. I was making enough on each share application to pay for a term of

Stagging

A 'stag' is a short term speculator who buys shares in a new issue with the intention of selling them at a profit as soon as dealing starts. Stags often try to buy as many shares as possible but in popular issues, the number of shares allocated to an individual tends to be small, so stags persuade others to apply for shares on their behalf. During the eighties, the rules against multiple applications began to be tightened up as stags made large profits, but in the early days of privatization there was little to prevent the quick-witted from exploiting the government's desire to ensure a successful share issue.

Table 1.1				
Company	Date	Issue price	Price day one	Premium
BAE	Apr 81	150p	171p	+14.0%
C& W	Nov 81	168p	198p	+14.0%
Amersham	Feb 82	142p	188p	+32.3%
Britoil	Nov 82	100p	81p	-19.0%
British Ports	Feb 83	112p	138p	+23.0%
Jaguar	July 84	165p	179p	+8.4%
BT	Nov 84	50p	90p	+80.0%
TSB	Sep 86	50p	85.5p	+71.1%
British Gas	Apr 81	150p	171p	+14%

school fees. Twenty applications paid for one child's entire education.

And it really was risk-free, almost. Only one of the issues lost money – Britoil, which dropped 19% on the first day of issue. You might think that was a serious loss, but my average first day gain on the others was 35%. 35% in one day!

By the spring of 1987 I wasn't feeling so clever, though. The privatized companies were doing well. Having cast off the shackles of state ownership, they were behaving as the free marketeers had predicted, becoming more efficient and more profitable. They had taken their share prices with them – see Table 1.2.

If I had held on to the shares instead of stagging them, I would have made a compound return of something like 80% a year, taking into account the various issue dates. I wouldn't have just

Table 1.2 April '87 Value of £1000 invested at issue	
Company	£
BAE	4213
C&W	2143
Amersham	3983
Britoil	1119
British Ports	4101
Jaguar	3606
BT	2131
TSB	1660
British Gas	1940
TOTAL	26519

made enough for the school fees; I could have bought the whole school!

That's how it looked to me in that City winebar in April 1987. Like most other people, I was new to the stock market, and it had done me proud. Since the war, the stock market had only really been for the professionals – the institutions and pension funds owned shares, not private individuals. Margaret Thatcher had created a whole new class of private share-owners, and we were new at the game.

The game itself wasn't new, of course, Joint stock companies appeared in Europe in the Middle Ages and the English got in on the act during the 1500s, when London merchants took a punt on voyagers like Sebastian Cabot, who sold six thousand pounds' worth of shares in twenty five pound lots to finance his

THE STREETWISE INVESTOR

attempt to find the Northeast Passage to the Orient. He failed to find it, but trade to Russia opened up with the founding of the Muscovy Company. Back in London, investors became ever more sophisticated as the Empire grew. That once-great insurance institution, Lloyd's of London, developed out of syndicates of coffee house patrons who had hedged their bets on shipping by parcelling up the risks and trading them between each other. There had been plenty of fraud, which is why some of the more honest brokers had left the coffee houses in the early 1800s to form their own investment club – which eventually became the London Stock Exchange.

Lloyd's of London

Lloyd's of London, the world's oldest insurance market, began in the 1600s as a coffee house where the shipping industry congregated. Gradually a system of maritime insurance developed there which was virtually the only kind of insurance in existence until the 1880s.

One of its unique characteristics is that it allows wealthy private individuals, known as 'Names', to underwrite insurance risks. In the late 1980s a series of natural disasters and large court awards to asbestosis victims in the US hit Lloyd's very badly, and many Names were ruined. Lloyd's began to reorganize itself, allowing corporations to become Names.

The terrorist attack in the US on the 11th of September 2001 hit Lloyd's very badly, costing it a record loss of £3 billion, but in 2002 Lloyd's was back in the black for the first time in six years, making a profit of £834m as insurance premiums soared.

8

All that *laissez-faire* free-marketeering had come to a halt after World War 2, so for most of us the stock market had been a closed book until Maggie Thatcher came along. She was determined to halt the tide of socialism and dependence on the state by making us take responsibility for our own assets. The trouble was, the state seemed to own almost everything and tax everything else out of existence, so there wasn't much incentive to take a risk.

Her solution was to provide incentives. She broke the unions, made it easier for firms to sack people, gave council house tenants the right to buy and made it easier to borrow money. Getting ordinary people to gamble on shares was a special challenge, but she found a way to do that too, by virtually eliminating the risk. There wasn't much chance of losing on a privatization issue because the government priced them low.

That was just to prime the pump – the government didn't want people just to stag the privatization issues and trouser the money. It wanted them to become committed stock market investors. It introduced all kinds of deals to encourage this, from lower taxes on share dealing to employee share schemes. It made the financial institutions feel confident that they could make money, made the big firms feel that they wouldn't be blackmailed by the likes of Arthur Scargill, and liberated the City with the Big Bang reforms. The stock market loved it. In 1985 the index stood at 900; by 1987 it had almost doubled. Suddenly there were millions of private shareholders slavering for a profit. A quarter of a million people turned up for the 'Money' Show at Olympia in London in 1986. You would expect that kind of turn-out for the Boat Show, but for a show about money? It was amazing and it didn't last. You could have got all the visitors to the Money Show of 2003 into my local village hall.

In 1987 the stock market was the only story in town. The market was rising so more new people were piling in, which led to the market rising even further. A lot of us were holding our breath, wondering how much longer it could last.

"You could float a brick in a cardboard box and people would buy it," said the man in the winebar and we had all laughed. Joining in the mirth, I couldn't help feeling that a crash wasn't far away.

Chapter 2

Black Monday, October 1987

It came when I wasn't looking. I took my eye off the ball for a couple of days and lost two million pounds. On Sunday I had popped over to Paris for a short break. On Tuesday I had an itch to check share prices and my whole world collapsed. Half my net worth had suddenly evaporated.

I felt suicidal. If the market continued to fall my portfolio might become worthless. How could I start out all over again at my age? Harry's Bar wasn't far away.

I tottered over there to drown my sorrows in beer with whisky chasers.

1987 had been quite a year. In May I had agreed to sell my company. It should have been a straightforward deal, but nothing is ever simple with a public company. We had to have an Extraordinary General Meeting (EGM) to get shareholders' approval even though the majority had already given irrevocable undertakings approving the deal. Rules are rules, so we had to wait for the EGM, which took until September. Meanwhile the company's share price had soared, hitting its all-time high in July.

Investment yardsticks

Trying to establish the 'true' worth of a company can never be an exact science, but investors use a variety of mathematical tools to help them decide whether or not shares are worth buying.

Here are three commonly used measures:

Yield – the dividend per share divided by the current share price. The current share price is the 'middle-price', which lies in the middle of the spread between the buy price and sell price.

If the share price is £2 and the net dividend is 5p, the net yield is $5/200 = 0.025$, or 2.5%.

Dividends are important because if you reinvest them in the company over a long period, they account for a large proportion of your total return. Historically in the UK market yields have generally been in the 4–6% range.

Price/earnings multiple (p/e, PE) – the current share price divided by the earnings per share.

If the share price is £2 and the earnings per share is 10p, the PE is $200/10 = 20$.

High PEs (over 14) mean that the market expects profit growth – but the market may be wrong. PEs are often high just before a market crash.

Book value (net asset value) – ordinary shareholders' funds (excluding intangible assets) divided by the number of shares in issue.

If the ordinary shareholders' funds are £100 million and there are 20 million shares, the book value is $100m / 20m = 5$. This would give a book value of £5 per share, which you then compare with the current share price.

> A warning – there are so many ways of calculating these apparently simple measurements that they can be very misleading. Make sure you are comparing like with like and don't be deceived by false precision; these yardsticks are only rough indicators.

During 1987 my firm's share price had gone up by more than half. Since its low in 1974, the price had risen twenty-fold. By July 1987 the yield was less than 3% and the price/earnings multiple was over 20. Looking back, it was obvious that something had to give.

When I'd finally sold in September, they handed me a document confirming my four million quid shareholding. I remember slipping it in my pocket as if it happened every day. A bit of paper worth £4 million. Nothing out the way.

I had sold myself along with the business, so I couldn't have flogged everything and gone sailing in the Med. I was locked in for five years as Chief Executive. That had seemed like a good idea, until the crash came. Sitting in Harry's Bar in Paris, I ordered a £600 bottle of Roederer Cristal champagne. What's another £600 when you have just lost £2 million? I wondered what to do next. Perhaps I could do a runner – sell my shares and leave the country. But then I'd be letting everyone down, including Sir John Harvey-Jones who had just come aboard as Chairman, having retired from ICI. I could get away with it, I supposed, but that would be the end of my business career. You can't let people down twice in the City.

The thought still appealed. My shares were still worth £2 million – how much is a good name worth? And for £2 million did I care?

I thought about the market. Of course it had been overvalued. Take Sock Shop, for instance. It came to the market in May '87, offering 18% of its equity at 125p per share, a prospective p/e of 24. That's steep by normal standards, but the issue was over-subscribed by 53 times. They only wanted £5 million and they had attracted £250 million. What did people think they were buying? Forty three shops – actually more like stalls than shops – that sold socks. It seemed daft to me, but I hadn't cared. I'd stagged it. On the first day of issue the share price opened at 205p. A couple of hours later it was at 290p. At the end of the day it closed at 257p, a prospective p/e of 50. I'd doubled my money in a day, which made losing half my net worth in two days seem almost reasonable.

Sock Shop was a conservative investment compared with Tie Rack, which floated a couple of weeks later. Tie Rack wanted to raise £12.5 million and was offering shares at a historic p/e of 31.5. It attracted £1 billion in share applications, an over-subscription of 85 times. The only surprise to me was that it attracted so little money. The p/e was high, but if you looked at Japan, where the average p/e was nearly 60, it didn't look so bad.

As I downed the last of the champagne, I tried to analyse what had happened. I'd thought we'd already had the necessary market 'correction' in August, when the market fell by 10%. By early October it had recovered and we had all relaxed. And now, with no warning, the market had derailed.

The Crash: July–November, 1987

From July to November the FTSE plunged:

	FTSE All Share Index	
16 July 1987	1238.57	
10 November 1987	784.81	Down 36.6%

The October crash is vividly remembered in City circles. It is probably the most widely remembered single post-war stock market event because it dominated the television, radio and newspaper headlines for several days. Just for once, there was a genuine air of menace behind the normally vacuous headlines about billions of pounds being written off stock market values when, on each of two successive days, the figure was £50 billion.

The October crash occurred in New York on Monday 19 October and in London on Monday and Tuesday, 19 and 20 October. Popularly assumed to be a crash from an all-time high, the stock markets had actually already peaked in July in London and August in New York. In London a sharp increase in the June trade deficit had an unsettling effect when it was announced on 22 July, and an unexpected increase in base rates on 6 August from 9% to 10% shook confidence by raising fears of recession. Further unease was caused by two large rights issues from WPP and Blue Arrow to finance ambitious transatlantic bids, and barely a month after reaching its peak of 1238.57 on 16 July, the All Share Index had fallen by 10% to 1114.81 on 20 August.

However over the next two months equities recovered to within sight of their peak in the first week of October. The All Share Index was 4% below its high on Friday 16 October, at which point the crash in London came to most people out of a clear blue sky – with the train hitting the buffers 'travelling flat out and fully loaded', as it was put at the time by Sir David Scholey, Chairman of S. G. Warburg Group.

The crash had its origins in New York. The chronology of events in New York is important to understand subsequent events in London. While London was falling away in July and August under the pressure of higher interest rates and a worsening trade deficit, Wall Street continued to race ahead to a peak in the Dow Jones Index of 2722.42 on 25 August before it paused to draw breath. Historic p/e ratios were over 20, dividends were around 2½%, and, in an indicator used more widely in New York than in London, share prices stood at a record 2½ times book value.

The market cracked on Tuesday 6 October when the Dow Jones Index suffered a 3.5% fall of 91.55 points to 2548.63 after the prime bank lending rate in New York was raised from 8¼ to 9¼. In the following week, the index fell away rapidly over three successive days after disappointing trade figures on Wednesday 14 October and another half-point increase in the prime rate to 9.75 on Thursday 15 October (see Table 2.1).

On the eve of the crash the Dow Jones had already fallen by 15% in 10 days in the face of the looming threat of recession and, in terms of points, had suffered its three largest ever one-day falls.

Table 2.2 Movements in the Dow Jones Index leading up to the market crash, October 1987				
Date in October	Dow Jones Index		Fall	
	From	To	points	%
Tuesday 6	2640.18	2548.63	91.55	3.5
Wednesday 14	2508.16	2412.63	95.46	3.8
Thursday 15	2412.70	2355.09	57.61	2.4
Friday 16	2355.09	2246.73	108.36	4.6

Worse still, this downward spiral was exacerbated by uneasy rumours in the market place about problems in Salomon Brothers, an aggressive investment bank widely regarded to be the leading bond trader on Wall Street. It was from among its ranks that Sherman McCoy might well have been drawn – the fictitious bond trader and so-called master of the universe, whose downfall is rivetingly portrayed in Tom Wolfe's novel *Bonfire of the Vanities.* With uncanny foresight this novel was written before the crash, as was the screenplay of the film *Wall Street* in which Michael Douglas vividly portrayed fictitious investment banker Gordon Gekko. Both vividly described the excesses of the 1980's and were surely warnings of the events to come.

Salomon Brothers had epitomized the long Wall Street bull market of the 1980's, and, in an uncontrolled expansion, its staff numbers had risen by 40% in the previous twelve months alone to a worldwide total of 6500. Salomon Brothers announced on Monday 12 October that, because business in the third quarter had been only 'marginally profitable' it was closing down segments of its trading operations and cutting staff numbers by 12%. This came as a shock to the Wall Street community. It sent out a signal clearly understood by the professionals in the investment banks and fund management world that the party was over. When professionals lose their collective nerve, the results for the public can be catastrophic.

Although in those final few days before the crash the London market was beginning to weaken, there was none of the sense of imminent danger pervading New York. The All Share Index fell on five consecutive days from Friday 9 October to Thursday 15 October, but only by some 2.4% overall. At this point fate played a strange hand. On the night of Thursday 15 October London and the South East of England suffered a devastating hurricane. London became inaccessible because so many trees had fallen on to roads and railway lines, and was rendered largely inoperable because of widespread power cuts and failed telephone exchanges. A few market makers made their way through trees and fallen masonry, only to put indicative prices to absent clients, and no indices were calculated. London was cut off from events from the moment prices were tumbling in New York after hours on the Thursday evening until the following Monday. Investors were thrown back to the conditions of an earlier century when news of momentous events in other capitals took a day or two to arrive and frustrated sellers were trapped.

Despite its New York origins, the crash actually began in London on Monday 19 October. Apart from Hong Kong the Asian and Australian markets had closed at lower levels, but not especially so and in Tokyo a 5% fall in Saturday trading had been partially recovered. In London the FTSE 100 lost 250 points, and the All Share Index fell by just under 10%. Dramatic this may have been, but as the global market moved westward to New York, it paled beside the unprecedented 22% fall of 508 points in the Dow Jones Index on a record turnover of 603 million shares, exacerbated by waves of automatic selling from computerized portfolio systems. It was from this single day in New York that the October crash achieved its fame and notoriety.

It caused the flood gates to open in the Far East the next morning – Tuesday 20 October – when the Nikkei Index in Tokyo fell by 12% and the Ordinary Index in Australia by 25%. The Hong Kong market was so overwhelmed with sellers that trading was suspended for the rest of the week, and when it reopened on 26

October the local Hang Seng Index recorded a net fall of 41%. The collapse continued as the clock moved round again to London where the indices recorded a fall of 11%, matching over two days the fall achieved in one day in New York. There it ended as New York recovered some of the lost ground with a 6% rise on the Tuesday. The cumulative percentage falls over the two days were as follows:

Hong Kong 40.7   Australia 27.8   UK-FTSE 21.7   USA 18.7

At the end of a gruelling week investors were numbed by uncertainty as the speed of the crash evoked memories of 1929, and for the next two week nerves would be tested to the limit by volatile markets continuing to fall. On Monday 26 October, the All Share Index fell by 7.2% and the FTSE 100 by 111.1 points to 1684.1. The next week was almost alarming as the crash itself as London went into its own daily freefall, and, over seven business days the All Share Index fell another 11.5%, taking the cumulative loss in just over three weeks to 34%.

These were painful days. Portfolio values had suffered grievously. At the time investors were genuinely frightened of an uncontrollable free fall comparable to that in 1929. Apart from brief setbacks in 1976 and 1079 investors had lived through a stunning bull market that had witnessed shares multiplying 20 times from 1975 to 1987. The sheer growth of the securities and fund management businesses over this period meant that only a minority of participants had experienced a proper bear market. The bewildered majority saw a third of their assets wiped out in three weeks.

The crash was the culmination of a universal drive into equities at unsustainable valuations. The difference between this and any previous crash was the common thread of global invest-ment, able to cross boundaries due to political deregulation, and easily implemented due to technology. The result was a global rush into equities without any safety valves to let down the inevitable head of steam. Indeed, technology itself accentu-ated the problem in Wall Street, when on the day of the crash an uncontrolled selling spiral was triggered by computer-pro-grammed portfolios. Computers chased each other downwards as each signal of falling prices triggered yet further sales.

What is 'War Loan'?

War Loan is a type of British Government stock (bond), which is essentially a loan from investors to the government.

It was issued during the First World War by Lloyd George and was often criticized because, unlike other stocks, it had no redemption date, which means that the government can choose when it pays the money back to the bondholders and may, in fact, never do so.

Today people are less worried about this aspect of War Loan stock, and there is healthy market in them, as there is for other types of UK Government stock (also called 'gilts').

Gilts pay out a fixed dividend, so the yield rises if a gilt falls in price and shrinks if it rises. Generally, gilts go up during times of uncertainty when investors prefer safety to higher returns.

Prices of gilts are published daily in the *Financial Times*. Each issue has a name comprising the title, the nominal yield and the redemption date, for example Treasury 8% 2003. They are divided into short-dated, where the redemption date is less than five years away, and groups of longer dated stocks.

Two years later, in 1989, I sold all my shares and got out of the market. I put the money into War Loan bonds which were paying 15%. It was one of those dream moments. Interest rates were very high and likely to go down; if they did, the market value of the bonds would soar. In the meantime I was getting a fixed rate of interest of 15%. How good was that? Good enough for me.

Chapter 3

New Age

Getting all your money out of the market gives you time to relax. I began to take an interest in other things. I encountered the 'New Age' and started wearing a pony tail. I read a lot more and began to develop a broader view of the financial markets. I told myself that I wouldn't speculate at all – unless there was something screamingly obvious.

War Loan bonds at 15% were screamingly obvious and they weren't speculative; I didn't have to watch the price all the time. I was out of the rat race and loving it. I didn't know where I was going or what I would do with the rest of my life, but it didn't matter. I was lucky and I knew it.

The dead cat bounce

Looking back at the October '87 crash, I realized how blind I had been at the time. I was in deep despair. If you had asked me about the market in early November 1987, I would have told you that it would take a decade for it to recover – there was no chance of the market bouncing back.

Shortly afterwards it bounced back by 11%. I was still bearish.

Dead cat bounce – a small rise in share prices after a very fast and drastic crash.

Base lending rate – the base lending rate is the interest rate that the Bank of England sets for lending to other banks. Everybody else pays more than the base rate, but it is used as the benchmark lending rate.

This was a 'dead cat bounce' if ever there was one, and I wasn't going to be seduced.

The 1988 Budget came as a surprise. Chancellor Lawson had a big give-away, with tax reductions for all and a big cut to the base lending rate. The top rate of tax was down to 40%, which was good news for the well-off. By the summer of 1988, the market had risen by another 10%, presumably because people were investing some of what they had saved from the taxman.

Everything began to look a little rosier – maybe there would be another boom. Then we got seven increases in the base rate in ten weeks. It went from 7.5% to 12%. People started handing the keys of their houses back to the building societies. Monthly trade deficits were at record highs and by November 1988 the base rate was at 13%. In the City, people were being sacked in droves. The market fell back to roughly where it was at the beginning of the year.

Looking at the fundamentals, the market was heading south. We had high interest rates, a weak pound, record balance of payment deficits and chaos in the financial services sector. If you were going to make a bet, you'd say that it would be a bear mar-

Trade deficit – this is when a country is importing more from abroad, in money terms, than it is exporting.

Fundamentals – a term used to describe the basic tests that investors use to value companies and judge how the economy will affect stock market prices. It is heavily based on numbers, and involves analysing elements such as sales, earnings, growth potential, debt management on the level of individual companies, whole industrial sectors and, more loosely, the entire economy.

ket in 1989 and sell the market short – it was the only rational thing to do. The market promptly went up by 30%, within a whisker of its all-time high.

It was as if nothing could keep it down. In October '89 the base rate went up to 15%, and the market fell back by 20%, and then ended the year back up again.

It was all a mystery to me, which was why all my money was in bonds. I was safe and free, but I couldn't help trying to understand why the market was behaving in the way that it did. It wasn't until I read John Littlewood's *The Stockmarket, 50 Years of Capitalism at Work* (Financial Times Professional Ltd 1998) that any of it began to make sense. Here's how he describes the period:

> No sooner had the market reached a new high in the first week of January than confidence rapidly evaporated. Consensus forecasts for the growth of the economy suggested a further slowing down from 5% in 1988 and 2.2% in 1989 to an estimate of 1.4% in 1990. Fears of inflation returned to

haunt investors when Ford workers rejected an offer of 10% in 1990, followed by 8% in 1991.

Signs of serious corporate strain emerged from previously glamorous sources. Coloroll - a wallcoverings and home products empire built aggressively in the 1980s by John Ashcroft – was found to be wallowing in debt with customers in retreat. In January a warning about profits and financing problems caused the shares to halve in price, and a company valued at £300 million at its peak was on the path to bankruptcy within 6 months. In February a leading property developer, Rosehaugh, suddenly announced a rights issue of crisis proportions to raise £125 million. Rosehaugh, trapped by high interest rates and falling rentals from Big Bang retrenchment – was also on the path from a market capitalization of £750 million to eventual bankruptcy, but the legacy of its visionary development of the Broadgate complex around Liverpool Street station remains for all to see.

The reporting season of the clearing banks revealed the scale of their continuing problems with Third World debt. Lloyds Bank reported a loss of £715 million, caused by writing down the amount of loans outstanding by £1,750 million, followed by Barclays adding a further £1,000 million to debt provisions, taking their total to £4,500 million. Meanwhile in Tokyo the Nikkei Index was in freefall – down 28% in 3 months to 28002.70 in the first week of April.

This series of gloomy headlines led to a 10% fall in the market in the first two months of the year, and a further 5% fall in April. The political and economic background was especially bleak for the Conservative Government. The Chancellor – Nigel Lawson – had resigned after a messy and damaging disagreement with the Prime Minister in October.

Labour held opinion poll leads of around 25%, the poll tax was deeply unpopular and house prices were stalling for the first time in a decade. Inflation was heading for double figures, trade deficits persisted and, in a mildly deflationary first budget on March 20th the new Chancellor – John Major – forecast growth of only 1% in 1990.

I was figuring that the worse the economic news got, the more my bonds would be worth, so in a way I was hoping for a market collapse, or at least a recession.

In August 1990 Iraq suddenly invaded Kuwait and all the major markets went into freefall. By mid-September the London stock exchange had dropped by 22%. If it dropped by another 20%, we would have been back at the lowest point of the 1987 crash.

Then Geoffrey Howe made his famous resignation speech attacking Margaret Thatcher. A few weeks later she was gone. What does the market do? It ends the year on its high for the year. I didn't know whether to laugh or cry.

The media said we had had enough of Thatcherite greed and what we wanted now was more caring and sharing. That suited me; I was changing nappies like a maniac and I had even planted a herb garden. I even started writing for the *Guardian* newspaper. That was very strange – in the 1980s I wouldn't have allowed the *Guardian* in my house, and now I had my own weekly column:

My pact with the Devil

Alan Moore recalls how he lost his soul and won a million
In 1963 . . . the year that intercourse began (though sadly not for me) . . . I played Mephistopheles to my own Faust and

after some debate I made a bargain with the Devil. Make me a millionaire by . . . let's say 40 at the latest . . . and as a bonus along the way, throw in as many women as I can handle (and let's not be too slow about it), and to Hell with my immortal soul, you can have it – good riddance to bad rubbish! Fuck the next world! For all I know there may not be one. No. It's this world that I care about; this life's riches and rewards I want.

And to seal the bargain, the next (and final) time I served Mass I stole three consecrated Hosts and nailed each one – Father, Son and Holy Ghost – to an inverted crucifix I made of balsa wood and Airfix glue. And I guess that even then I'd hoped they'd bleed . . .

In the City the Eighties were one long hard-on, everybody had the horn –every thrusting merchant banker; every double-dealing broker; every hard-nosed limp-dicked lawyer (yes, even they could get it up) – and they weren't too fussy who they screwed. Clients came. Clients went. Here today and screwed tomorrow. It was all the same to them, they didn't give a fuck . . . not unless you paid them.

And was this frenzy all about reshaping British business? Forget it. Size! Who could pull off the biggest deals? Who could command the biggest fees? Who had the biggest cock in town? That's what it was all about. And in the summer of '87 I though I had . . . I really did . . . and that now all I had to do was to prove it. Which just goes to show – yes, you've said it – what a stupid prick I was.

Stupid maybe; but I did at least have some credentials – a £50 million public company, £10 million in cash and far more importantly, the essential sky-high share price. And at least I understood the rules; I knew what game we were playing; I knew what we had to do – and the first thing was to find a target, a company we could take over cheaply using our highly rated shares; a company preferably far larger than ourselves. And as it happened we knew just the one . . .

By October our plans were well advanced. We'd worked out we could go as high as £50 million and not dilute our earnings and at that price we were confident we would win. Everything looked set. I decided to take a few days off before the action began. I left for France on Sunday 18th and motored down to stay with friends in the Loire for a couple of days before heading for Paris and the Ritz – an old favourite – from where I called my secretary . . . and when I put the phone down I was only half the man I'd been.

Two days! That's all I'd been away. And in that time I'd lost £2 million half of all I had. It wasn't possible. It couldn't happen. Not to me. Not to Alan Moore. There must be some mistake. Only there wasn't: markets around the world had crashed on an unprecedented scale, our shares had halved, the deal was off and I was now the chief executive of a £20 million company.

I flew back to an emergency board meeting. There wasn't much to be said. The game was over – that much was obvious – and all that was left was a rather nasty, sticky mess. And I remember thinking – well, it had to happen sometime: there had to be a price. And somewhere in my heart of hearts I thought I'd got off lightly.

I was right, I had, but not for long. A few months later on a dark forest path something unseen spooked my nine year-old daughter's horse, and as she lay helpless on the ground, she was stamped on in the face and suffered dreadful injuries, including the loss of her left eye. And even then I didn't see. Not at first. Then as I watched her bravely struggle with the pain of not one, but 13 operations I began to see things differently: to ask myself what was important. It was as if her loss had given me the gift of sight – a third eye, if you like. An eye with which to see the truth. My truth.

And what I saw I didn't like. I saw a vain and hollow man who was a pretty worthless individual; a man who though outwardly successful, inwardly despised himself. A man whose life, a long way back, had taken a wrong and almost fatal turning. A man who had no idea who he really was.

A few months later I resigned. My business career was at an end. I could not continue. I had been lost too long. The time had come to find a way back to myself.

A few days later I took stock of my finances; what with the falling stock market and various tax liabilities I wasn't sure what I still had left. It was a complicated calculation and when I finished and saw the figure I kept the piece of paper. I have it here. The net total is £3,017,500. Next to it I've added – "Call it £1 million". A few days later I was 40.

So I had changed, both as a person and in my attitude towards the markets. I felt that I had a better grasp of reality, and this was to stand me in good stead when the next boom came along – the so-called 'New Economy'.

Chapter 4

The New Economy mania

Ten years later, everyone seemed to have forgotten about the crash of '87. I was sitting out one of the biggest stock market booms in history. The higher it went, the better I liked it. At its peak the market would offer what was, without doubt, the biggest money-making opportunity in stock market history. I was waiting for the bubble to burst.

And burst it did.

The market peaked on the last trading day of the decade – and of the millennium. It was bizarre; why was everyone buying on that day? It was as if they were expecting the Second Coming in the year 2000.

Something came, alright, but it wasn't paradise on earth.

Investors warned to shelter from "dot bombs."
Insiders believe many internet companies are over-valued and the bubble is about to burst.

(*Financial Times*, 3 February 2000)

When even a Silicon Valley insider calls internet stocks 'a bubble', UK investors should take note.

IPOs

An Initial Public Offering, or IPO, is simply the US term for a new issue, when a company first offers its shares to the public on the stock market. Companies have choices about how they will issue their shares and may decide on a 'private placing', when shares are offered exclusively to financial institutions and favoured private clients.

During the internet boom small American investors became frustrated at being kept out of private placings of technology shares, so demand grew for IPOs and the term acquired an undeserved glamour. The privatization issues of the Thatcher era were IPOs, but the term wasn't widely used in Britain at the time.

As much as half the $400bn (£243.90bn) combined valuation of US dot-coms is due to market hype and investor naivety, claims Tony Perkins, co-owner of Red Herring, the California-based bible for dot-com investors.

The attack is all the more unexpected because it bears the hallmarks of an inside job: the authors have been at the centre of the dot-com investment phenomenon. "We could see from our position how the market was stacked against the small-time investor and outsider," said Mr Perkins, co-author of The Internet Bubble, published in the UK this week. "If I have a warning for UK investors, it is don't follow the herd."

The authors also argue that traditional evaluation techniques such as price/earnings multiples should apply to dot-coms.

Some analysts have argued that internet companies

should be measured by different yardsticks such as their market share or by calculating the individual valuation of each web customer based on forecast revenues. Many web companies, such as Amazon.com, have explicitly vowed to sacrifice short-term profits in order to build market share.

However The Internet Bubble believes divorcing valuations from earnings has inflated the "bubble" stocks. The book will add to the debate over how to value internet stocks, particularly with a rush of UK IPOs expected by dot-coms this spring. It argues that the soaring market capitalisations experienced by floated dot-coms, on both sides of the Atlantic, are produced by many factors. These include the higher valuations placed on companies at earlier stages by venture capitalists, the limited number of shares made available in public dot-coms and the impact of non-professional investors such as day and online traders.

But the biggest factor is greed.

"The fact is most non-professional investors cannot buy shares before an IPO because the investment banks that underwrite flotations keep most of the stock back for their customers. The only way a small-time trader can get involved is often when the share price has already been dumped by the mutual funds and the VCs. They are buying at the highest point. This explains the incredible jump in the first day valuations of IPO shares."

"The venture capitalists and investment banks always walk away with their money from the dot 'bombs'. It's the little guy that is getting burnt."

You can say that again! Opportunists were making fortunes out of companies that looked virtually worthless by any conventional valuation method and an army of analysts were preaching the 'New Economy' doctrine that was supposed to explain why the sky-high prices were actually still a bargain.

I'd learned a lot about the market since 1987 and acquired some new techniques. I knew now that you can make even more money when the market is going down than when it is going up – if you have the right investment tools. Why should a falling market be better? It's simple: markets tend to fall much faster than they rise. The gains of several years can by wiped out in a few days. The trick is to catch the crash and 'short' the shares, which is what I was hoping to do when the Internet bubble finally burst.

Every investor has heard about 'shorting' – essentially, making a bet that a share price will drop – but it hasn't been easy for non-professionals to do it in practice, especially in Britain. If you can't find a broker who will help you to short, you can't do it, so if the market drops your only options are to sit tight or bale out as quickly as possible.

Even in a rising market, share prices still spend almost as many days going down as going up. It's a greasy pole – you climb up three feet, drop back by two, then climb up again. As I read more about stock market history, I became acutely aware of how vulnerable the ordinary punter is in a bear market. People buy shares in the hope that they will go up and then have to sit there, sometimes for years, watching the prices sink.

Tech Stocks In Turmoil

The pleasures and the pain in a year of market mania: The visionaries of the high-tech revolution seemed invincible. Investors, afraid of being left out of the telecoms and dotcom boom, rushed to give them money.

And then the bubble burst.

(*Financial Times*, 23 December 2000)

The irrepressible Jeff Bezos, chairman of Amazon.com, knows the pain of running a company that has fallen out of favour in the financial world.

His creation, the biggest retailer on the Web, could well have doubled its sales by the time the year ends. But Mr Bezos' personal fortune, tied to his one-third stake in Amazon, has shrunk by $10bn as the company's shares have plummeted. "It has been a great business year and a terrible stock market year," he muses. The second part, at least, is something that few would dispute.

This will go down as a year in which more stock market wealth was destroyed than ever before. And a large chunk of that has been in technology and telecommunications – industries which started the year in triumphalist mood.

The Nasdaq market, home to many of the biggest US tech companies, has lost more than $3,000bn in value since its peak in March – more than three times the gross domestic product of China.

Stock markets around the world have felt the tremors from Nasdaq's almighty stumble. Germany's Neuer Markt, Europe's fledgling market for technology companies, hardly had a chance to establish itself before trouble struck. It is now 70 per cent off its peak.

It was the end of a classic stock market bubble. Like other technology-driven investment booms of the past – such as the early days of the railroads – the mania for information technology was founded on a wonderful vision. This technological revolution would have profound social and economic consequences, changing everyday life in ways that were not yet imaginable – and creating wealth that could only be dreamed of.

The bubble burst this year in two stages. The first setback was the most dramatic, but the second will turn out to be the most far-reaching.

Phase one was the spring collapse of the dotcoms. The intangible nature of this promise was part of its appeal. Dotcom companies that dared to dream of new internet-based commercial markets with instant worldwide reach, or telecoms companies that set out to build new global networks from scratch, found money easy to come by. They did not need to prove their ideas would work, only that they had a compelling vision.

Investors lined up to hand them money in the biggest wave of initial public offerings ever seen. And once share prices started going up, nobody wanted to be left out. Afraid of missing the boat, private and institutional investors alike drove tech and telecom stocks up by 100 per cent in the final six months of the mania.

The internet may end up changing the world, but investors woke up suddenly to the realisation that many dotcoms would never make any money from this revolution.

Phase two was a more agonising market slide that began in September – a decline that has reached out to most corners of the tech and telecoms world. And with signs that the world's biggest growth industry could be facing a severe slowdown, the slide may not be over yet.

Looking back, the broad sequence of events was so drearily predictable. First the real rubbish – the dotcoms – went, and then the telecom companies, who had become greedy at the prospect of the world's population being permanently glued to their mobile phones and had overpaid for their licences. The rot was spreading to the main markets now. The FTSE 100 was off its peak by 15% at this stage. It dropped another 25% during the next nine months.

America had been mad for all kinds of technology, not just the internet, and most of the new firms were quoted on NASDAQ. In November 1999 the London Stock Exchange created its own technology index, Techmark, so that high-tech fans could track what was going on over here. They could hardly have picked a worse time to do it. What happened next wasn't pretty at all.

Just look at Figure 4.1! In the first four months Techmark shot up by nearly 150%, and then over the next three months it dropped back most of the way. You might expect that from some wildly speculative start-up company, but this was the whole sector. It included well-known giants like British Telecom, Amstrad, Vodaphone and Reuters, firms at the cutting edge of the tech-

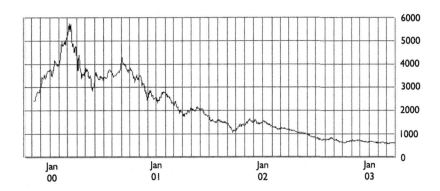

Figure 4.1 Techmark index, 2000–2003

nology that is supposed to be shaping our future. By the end of 2001 Techmark was back where it started and heading south. It was enough to make you weep – unless you knew how to short. Even better than that is knowing how to win whichever way the market goes.

To my mind, life's too short to be a long-term investor. If you have the right investment tools, you don't need to wait for ten years to make some money and you don't have to pick the right companies. With the right tools, you can make money out of the lame ducks, the fraudsters, the victims and the dinosaurs as well as from the stars. I'm going to show you how to do it; that's what the rest of this book is about.

Chapter 5

Introducing the Contract for Difference

Every fantastic new product needs a snappy name. What would you do if you had come up with an incredible new trading concept that makes buying stocks and shares in the traditional way almost entirely redundant – would you call it a 'Contract for Difference'?

Talk about lack of imagination! Would Elton John have become a star if he had stayed with the name on his birth certificate: Reg Dwight? The Contract for Difference (CFD) is the Reg Dwight of the investment world. It's an incredible product suffering from a lacklustre name. I expect someone will rename it eventually, but in the meantime I've privately re-christened the CFD as 'Elton'.

CFDs have been around since the mid-nineties but not many people have heard of them. Five years ago they were very limited. You could only use CFDs to trade in a handful of shares, which put a lot of people off. Since then the market has matured and the range of CFDs has exploded. Today, you can use CFDs to trade any UK listed firm with a market capitalization of over £50 million pounds and any firm listed in Europe or the US with a market capitalization of over 500 million euros or dollars respectively. You can also use CFDs to trade all the major currencies, commodities, futures and global stock indices, which pretty much covers everything most people would want to invest in.

As I mentioned in the last chapter, before CFDs came along a small private investor – what they call a 'retail investor' – had a lot of difficulty in betting that a share price might drop. The only way you could make money was if the market was rising and you bought a share that went up. With CFDs, you can make money if a share price goes down and, better still, if it goes up and down like a yo-yo.

Yes, of course you can lose money! CFDs are at the higher risk end of the investment spectrum. You still have to get it right.

The way I see it, you can get it right if you trust what you know. You don't have to get every trade right, just enough of them to come out winning. To me, it's about tuning in and making your intuition work for you.

Making the difference

So what's so different about CFDs? Let's look at the main benefit:

It doesn't matter whether the price goes up or down.

When you buy a share you do so in the hope that over a period of time the price will rise. If it does you can sell at the higher price and make a profit. Conversely, if the price falls you stand to make a loss. Plainly everything depends on the share going up. In the majority of cases this will in turn depend on the market as a whole going up; certainly over a sustained period of time it

Sectors – a sector is simply a way of categorizing companies into groups of similar businesses. This is a useful to compare the nature and performance of different industries, but it can be misleading. While it may be sensible to lump, say, all mining companies together into a sector, or all food retailing chains, newer industries are less predictable, so some very dissimilar companies may be grouped together in the same sector. Don't make the mistake of assuming that sector analysis is a precise way of defining and measuring industries.

Stocks or shares? – Traditionally in Britain the word 'stock' was used to mean what the Americans call 'bonds'. Confusingly, Americans call shares 'stocks'. These days we are so used to American terminology that many people use the terms 'shares' and 'stocks' interchangeably to mean 'shares'. Usually it is clear from the context whether or not they mean 'shares' or 'bonds' when they say 'stocks'.

will. From this it follows that there will be periods of time when losses are inevitable because the market is sinking.

With CFDs it does not have to be like that. A fall in the share price can still give you a gain. If you think a share is going up you can take out a CFD, and if you think a share is going down you can take out a contract. If you prefer, you can take out CFDs on the market as a whole, or on sectors of the market, such as technology or retailing.

Even better, you are not confined only to the UK market. Before CFDs, retail investors found it difficult to deal in shares listed on foreign exchanges, principally because of a lack of brokers who would handle the business and higher transactions costs. We're living in a global economy now, and we should take advantage of it. If you think that Wall Street is heading for a fall, you can take out a CFD. If you think that the Japanese market is due for a rise, you can take out a CFD.

Suppose you have done very well out of a share that has risen 60% and you think it is due for a 'correction', which is a polite way of saying a fall in price. As well as selling your holding for a 60% profit, you can also take out a CFD betting on a fall in price (a 'down' contract) in the hope of more profits if you are correct and the price does drop.

Up is good, but down is even better

Since the dot-com bust we have seen a period of almost continually falling markets, so it has been a good time to go short. In my experience it is often better to go short than long even in a static or rising market because of other factors:

1. Sharp falls

While rises in share prices tend to take place over long periods of time, price falls, following events such as a profit-warning, can be both instant and severe. An instant fall means an instant profit.

2. It's easier to tell when a share is too expensive

I believe that overvalued companies are generally easier to spot than undervalued ones. Indeed there often comes a point when a share price is soaring when anyone except a lunatic would agree that it is too high – in other words, that you are paying far more for your little piece of the company than it is actually worth. Why would a share price ever each that point? Nobody really knows, but it's probably often because investors are applying the 'bigger fool theory'. The 'bigger fool theory' means hoping that someone is a bigger fool than you are and is going to take your overpriced share off your hands. You know that the share price is unsustainable, but you are hanging on a bit longer in the hope that the price goes up even more. At some point the dam breaks, everyone starts selling and the price collapses – you're hoping you get out just before that happens.

3. It's harder to tell when a share is too cheap

Undervalued shares are hard to assess. Even if you find one, I think it would be rarely at an insanely low valuation. It might be trading at a p/e of perhaps one-half to one-third of its realistic valuation. That isn't bad, but a grossly overvalued company is often trading at a p/e that is much higher than the market averages. If it hasn't made a profit, it won't even have a p/e. If that sounds crazy, just look back at all those dot com companies that had no profits and no p/e.

4. New crazes often end in tears

Many of the most overvalued companies are new companies in exciting industries that are yet to make a profit. Investors often value hope more highly than reality, and often the price starts to fall at the moment when a firm declares its first profit. The reality of the company's situation begins to sink in and investors start to lose their rose-tinted spectacles.

Bull and bear markets – nobody is quite sure how the terms 'bull' and 'bear' came to be used in the stock market, but they probably first appeared in the US in the 1800s. A 'bull' is someone who thinks that prices are going up, and a 'bear' is someone who thinks prices are going down. By extension, a 'bull market' is one where prices keep rising, and a 'bear market' is when they keep dropping.

Short and long – going 'long' means investing your money in a security in the hope of a price rise, while going 'short' means taking a bet that the price will drop.

Derivatives – derivatives have been around for a very long time (at least since the Middle Ages) and they come in all shapes and sizes. Unlike shares and bonds, they are not based on a tangible asset, but are promises between two parties regarding 'underlying' assets such as shares, bonds, currencies, commodities and so on. For instance, a share option gives you the right to buy or sell a share at a certain price within a fixed time period – but it is not the same thing as the share itself.

Timing your trades

Now for the hard part. You have spotted an opportunity where a share price is either overvalued or undervalued. The question is, when should you take out a CFD? You may be right about the price, but do you know when the price 'correction' is going to happen? It could take months, even years. Everything tells you it's going to happen, that it must happen eventually, but you don't know when

That is the problem with a lot of futures contracts. The contract runs for a set period, such as a day, a month or three months and then expires. Sod's Law being Sod's Law, the correction will happen after your contract has expired.

CFDs are open-ended – they don't expire at the end of a fixed time period. I don't think enough is made of this benefit. Before CFDs I was always getting timed out on futures contracts. For me the fact that CFDs are open-ended was one of the major advantages that attracted me to them in the first place. Several years and several thousand trades later I see no reason to revise this opinion.

Coping with margin trading

When you buy a share you have to pay for it. If you buy 10,000 pounds' worth of shares it is going to cost you £10,000 plus transaction charges. CFDs are different. If you open a £10,000 CFD position, you are usually only going to have to put up a 10% 'margin', which is £1,000. This is trumpeted as a significant advantage, as indeed it is. It means that £1,000 deposited with a CFD provider can be used to open positions to the value of £10,000. Similarly a £5,000 deposit can be used to open positions to the value of £50,000.

It's always nice to borrow money, but it can be dangerous. Suppose you deposit £5,000 with your CFD broker and open positions to the value of £50,000. You potentially stand to lose £50,000, in which case your £5,000 would have disappeared and your broker would want another £45,000 from you. A more likely scenario is that your CFD positions go against you by 10%, and you lose the £5,000 you deposited. If your CFD positions went against you by 20%, you would have lost the £5,000 you deposited and owe the broker another £5,000.

For this reason CFDs are rightly perceived as risky. The Financial Services Authority (FSA) rules say that in order to open a CFD account, you have to satisfy the CFD provider that you are a suitable person to trade in CFDs. In other words, that you properly understand the risks.

It's one of the strange things about life that there are many people out there who cannot get their heads around risk. Maybe they were spoiled as children. Maybe they are just neurotic. You know the type – they are the bad losers at board games, the ones that throw the chess pieces off the table when you say "Checkmate". Lots of retail investors are like that – just ask any stock broker.

In fact, one of the most interesting fields of study in experimental psychology today is the research into how people misperceive risk. Apparently most of us do, grossly, unless we train ourselves not to.

Business and investing is all about being good at assessing risk. That's how you spot a bargain. Suppose nobody will buy a certain house because there's a scary-looking problem with the roof. You go along with some experience and you assess the cost of putting the roof right. You do your sums and decide that the house is still a bargain. If you are correct, you make money.

Conversely, people are often willing to take crazy risks if they are presented in an attractive way. That's how lotteries work. The odds are terrible, but what if you were that person who won two million quid last week? Every week millions of people around the country chuck money away buying lottery tickets at terrible odds. Many of them can't afford it – so you can see why the FSA doesn't want people like that getting themselves into trouble with trading CFDs on margin.

If you are reading this book you may well be reasonably good at assessing risk. You may not have studied it formally, but you have a grasp of the basic principles. My advice is, keep learning about it. Dig out some maths books and go over basic probability and statistics. Read some investment textbooks and learn about the academic research into how the stock market may or may not behave. Don't get too carried away, though. Most investing isn't rocket science; common sense will take you a very long way indeed.

A lot of stock market traders talk about the need for 'character' and 'discipline'. What they mean is, always try to assess the risks as carefully as you can. Some people get overexcited when they trade on margin and forget that if things go wrong they will have to pay up. You need to have 'character' – if you lose £100,000 that you don't have, you are going to be in trouble, so don't take the risk.

When you open a CFD position with a small deposit, think of the total amount you are putting at risk. If you deposit £5,000 and have open positions to the value of £50,000, you have £50,000 at risk, just as you would if you bought £50,000 of shares. If you don't understand this, you have no business trading CFDs or anything else except very small quantities of chocolate buttons.

The fact that you only have to put up £5,000 to take a £50,000 risk is irrelevant. It's convenient, maybe, but that's all it is.

Except for the occasional disaster, in practice the risk is unlikely to be 100%, just as if you had bought £50,000 worth of shares you would not generally expect to lose the whole lot – but it can and does happen sometimes. Look at Marconi, a once-great British firm that got well and truly ruined by new management and lost more than 99% of its value at the end of the dot-com bust.

Before opening any position I assess the risks in relation to the full value of the contract. What is important is to look at the potential downside, work out much you are prepared to lose and effect the contract accordingly. If you assess the downside at 20% and you are prepared to lose £10,000, then a £50,000 contract is fine. If you assess the downside at 20% but don't want to lose more than £2,500, then take out a £12,500 contract.

Limiting the risk

The current risk of terrorist attacks and the like is adding to the normal risks of equity investment. No matter how careful you are at picking your shares, events entirely outside your control can make things go horribly wrong. If you buy shares in the conventional way there is little you can do about it, but when you trade CFDs using a Limited Risk facility you can decide on the degree of risk you are prepared to accept.

In return for a small addition to the normal commission you can limit your potential losses to an agreed and guaranteed figure by using stop-loss instructions. We'll look at how stop-loss works in the next chapter.

No Stamp Duty

If you buy shares in the conventional way, you pay 0.5% Stamp Duty. It doesn't seem very much if you only buy occasionally, but if you start trading frequently it starts to add up. If you traded £25,000 worth of shares every day, over the course of a year you would pay more than £25,000 in Stamp Duty.

CFDs are derivatives and are free of Stamp Duty.

CFDs and longer-term investing

People often say that CFDs are appropriate for short-term trading but are no good if you want to hold on to your shares for a long time. They base their argument on the fact that you have to pay interest on the margin you are using – the 90% that you are effectively borrowing from the CFD provider – when you open your position.

Suppose you open a 'long' (buy) contract. While the contract remains open any dividends due will be credited to your account. Against this interest on the money you have borrowed will be debited on a daily basis. Rates vary from provider to provider, but it is normally about 2.5% over base rate.

Ignoring dividends and commission, let's compare a £10,000 purchase of the actual shares against a £10,000 CFD trade in the same shares and see where we are after 12 months:

	£10,000 share purchase		£10,000 CFD trade
Cost (£)	10,000	Margin (£)	1,000
Stamp Duty	50		–
Loss of interest on £10,000 at, say, 3% net	300	Interest paid on £10,000 at 6% gross	600
		Loss of interest on £1,000 margin at, say, 3% net	30
Total	10,350		1,630

Adjusting for the interest you lose when you make a purchase rather than keeping the money on deposit, the CFD interest is not so great. In this example, after 12 months the additional cost of the CFD is £280 or some 2.8%. This assumes that you are only getting a 3% net return on the £9,000 you have not had to lay out, which may be overly conservative. If you were getting a 6% net return the picture is very different.

Personally, in the current economic climate I feel it is worth paying the CFD interest and keeping my cash on deposit, free to be put to other uses. If inflation and interest rates were to soar, the picture might be very different. Over longer periods of time, say a decade or more, major changes are likely to occur, such as recessions, wars, regulatory changes and tax reforms that could make it too expensive to keep the CFD.

Holding a CFD position open for a year or two is not exactly long-term investment, but it is certainly a lot longer than day trading and, in my view, it's worth the cost.

Contracts for Difference: Summary		
Considerations	Buying Shares	Trading CFDs
Profit from falling prices	✗	✓
Can limit risk	✗	✓
Deposit only	✗	✓
No Stamp Duty	✗	✓
Long-term investment	✓	✓

To put it in a nutshell, give me 'Eltons' any day.

Chapter 6

How to use contracts for change

In the last chapter we saw that trading CFDs offers significant advantages when compared to buying shares in the traditional way. Personally, I think that these advantages are so strong that it is hard to make a case for ever trading the underlying stock. It's a radical view, but it is my personal experience that this is the case.

The great thing about CFDs – apart from all the other great things – is that they are simple, like me. I have my own way of doing things; it may not be clever, but so what? You don't have to be clever. Forget all the rocket scientists, the teenage scribblers, the masters of the universe and all the other market whiz-kids. You don't need them. All you need is yourself, CFDs and a working knowledge of how to use them.

Contracts for Difference offer you all the benefits of trading shares without having to physically own them. Simply put, a CFD is a contract that mirrors the performance of a share or index. It is traded on margin and just as with physical shares your profit or loss is determined by the difference between the opening and closing price of the contract.

Using stop-loss

Some CFD providers offer a stop-loss facility that enables you to cap your potential losses at a figure you feel comfortable with. For example, if you deposit £10,000 and make a £100,000 trade with a 10% stop-loss then if the worst happens and it goes against you, you get 'stopped out' when you have lost £10,000, which is 100% of your deposit.

The first thing to ask yourself before making a trade is how much you are prepared to lose if it goes wrong. If the answer is less than the minimum deposit required, don't open the position. If you're only prepared to lose £10,000, don't deposit £20,000.

There is a psychological 'trade-right' zone that keeps you on your toes. If you have too little at stake, you won't care if you lose, and you may lose your focus. If you have too much at stake, your fear will affect your judgement. Your 'trade-right' zone is the size of the deposit that makes you pay attention while keeping calm. If you have bet too much or too little, you're outside the 'trade-right' zone. Either way, when you are outside the zone, you are likely to lose money. If it is any comfort, I have tried both and lost badly. I could write a book called 'Fifty ways to lose your money in derivatives'. So could a lot of other people.

Get used to gearing

'Gearing' – which the Americans call 'leverage' – means increasing your potential gains and losses by using borrowed money. If you have made money out of selling your house, you almost certainly benefited from gearing. For example, if you bought a house for 50,000 with a 10% deposit, you borrowed 45,000 from a mortgage lender. If house prices rose by 20% and you then sold the house for 60,000, you made a profit of 10,000 before expenses, which is twice your initial deposit, or a return of 200%. That's a fabulous return, which is why everyone loves houses. Notice that the actual price of the house only went up by 20% – it was the effect of using borrowed money (gearing) that gave you your 200% return. If you had bought the house for 100% cash, you would only have made a 20% return.

The difference between house-trading and CFDs is that you can't buy and sell houses rapidly, and there are all kinds of regulations to protect you during the bad times in the housing market cycle, so most people manage to survive a drop in house prices. With CFDs on the other hand, you can be wiped out very quickly . . .

If you buy £10,000 of shares in the conventional manner, that's how much you pay (plus transaction costs). As we have seen, if you open a £10,000 CFD position you will only have to put up an initial deposit (margin) of between 5 and 20% (£500–2,000). The deposit amount required depends on the particular stock or index traded. That gives you a gearing effect – if you have deposited £10,000 and you make a 20% return on your £100,000, your profit is £20,000, which is a huge return on the £10,000 cash that you actually had to deposit. The flip side is that if you lose 20% on your £100,000 and you have lost £20,000, your £10,000 deposit has gone, plus you owe a further £10,000. So remember to reduce your risks by using stop-losses!

Going long

If you believe the price of a particular share or index is likely to rise and you want to bet on it, you effect a buy contract. This is known as 'going long'. If you have a long position your account is debited to reflect interest adjustments and credited to reflect any dividends. The effect of these adjustments is to mirror the economic effects of buying shares in the normal way, where you no longer earn interest on the money spent on the shares, but receive dividends instead.

Here's an example to show how this works:

Example 1: Buying Debenhams

Opening the position

It is early April and you decide that Debenhams is looking cheap. The share price is 320/322p in the market. You buy 10,000 shares as a CFD at 322p, the offer price.

The commission on the transaction is 0.25% or £80 (10,000 shares × 322p × 0.25%). There is no stamp duty to pay.

10,000 shares:	£32,200
Commission:	£80

Interest adjustments

While your position remains open your account is debited to reflect interest adjustments and credited to reflect any dividends. Each day, interest is calculated on the 'daily closing value' of the position. The 'daily closing value' is the number of shares multiplied by the closing price.

Suppose that on one day in mid-April the interest rate is 6% and the closing price of the shares on a particular day is 330p.

The closing value of the position is

10,000 shares $\times$ 330p = £33,000

The interest cost for this particular day is

£33000 $\times$ 6%/365 = £5.42

Each day's interest will probably be different.

Dividend adjustment

In early May your position is still open. Debenhams pays a dividend. The amount of the net dividend is 6.5p per share and this is credited to your account:

10,000 shares $\times$ 6.5p = £650

Closing the position

By late May Debenhams has risen to 365/368p in the market. You decide to take your profit. You sell 10,000 shares at 365p, the bid price.

The commission on the transaction is 0.25% or £87 (10,000 shares x 365p x 0.25%)

Your profit on the trade is:

Closing price   365p
Opening price   322p

Difference   43p

Profit on trade   43p × 10,000 = £4,300

That £4,300 is your 'gross profit' on the contract for difference. You now have to deduct all the costs from it and add any income:

You paid two sets of commission: 80 +87 = £167

Say you held the position for 50 days; with interest at 6%, your total interest charge might be: £282

On the plus side, you received a dividend: £650

Your total profit is:

Profit on trade	£4,300
Less commission	(£167)
Less interest adjustment	(£282)
Plus dividend adjustment	£650
Overall profit	£4,501

Going short

If you believe that the price of a particular share or index is likely to fall you can effect a 'sell contract'. This is known as 'selling short'. If you have a short position your account is credited to reflect interest adjustments and debited to reflect any dividends.

Here's how this works in practice.

Example 2: Selling Debenhams short

Opening the position

It is now October. Debenhams have powered ahead and are now in the market at 445/448p. You believe they are now over-bought and are due for a correction. You sell 10,000 shares as a CFD at 445p, the bid price.

The commission on the transaction is 0.25% or £111 (10,000 shares × 445p × 0.25%). There is no stamp duty to pay.

Because you have taken a short position your account is credited to reflect interest adjustments and debited to reflect any dividends.

Interest adjustments

The interest credit on your position is calculated daily by applying the applicable interest rate to the daily value of the position.

In this example the applicable interest rate might be 2% and the closing price of the shares on a particular day might be 438p, giving a closing value of £43,800 (10,000 shares × 438p).

The interest credit for the position for this particular day would be £2.40 (£43,800 × 2%/365).

Dividend adjustment

In November your position is still open at the time of the Debenhams ex-dividend date. The amount of the net dividend is 5p a share and this is debited to your account. The adjustment is calculated as:

10,000 shares × 5p = £500

Closing the position

By early December Debenhams has fallen back to 405/407p in the market and seems to be resistant to going below 400p. You decide to close your position and take your profits. To close out, you buy 10,000 shares at 407p, the offer price. The commission on the transaction is 0.25% or £102 (10,000 shares × 407p × 0.25%).

Your profit on the trade is calculated as follows:

Opening level	445p
Closing level	407p
Difference	38p
Profit on trade	38p × 10,000 = £3,800

Calculating the overall result

To calculate the overall profit on the transaction you have to take account of the commission you have paid together with all the interest and dividend.

In this example you might have held the position open for 48 days, earning a total interest credit of say, £112. Against this you have been debited £500 in respect of the dividend.

The overall result of the trade is a profit calculated as follows:

Profit on trade	£3,800
Commission	(£213)
Interest adjustment	£112
Dividend adjustment	(£500)
Overall profit	£3,199

Since you 'lose' the dividend when you are a short seller, it is always important to check the date of the next dividend payment so you know when this is coming – sometimes it may be worth closing the position just before the dividend is due.

Summary of interest and dividends

The way interest and dividends are calculated is a bit confusing at first, so let's go over it again:

- When you are short, the calculation of dividends and interest is the opposite of when you are long.

- For long (buy) positions, dividends are credited and interest is debited.

- The interest rate charged varies depending on the CFD provider to provider, but is typically 2–2.5% over base rate. Since dividends are credited, which offsets the interest, the costs of running long-term buy positions in shares that pay good dividends are greatly reduced. Many shares are currently yielding 6–7% dividends, which would cover all your interest costs.

- For short (sell) positions, dividends are debited and interest is credited.

- The interest you receive is typically 2–2.5% *below* the base rate. Since dividends are debited it is important to take this into account before you open the position. If you are shorting a share that pays little or no dividend this problem does not occur.

Limited risk protection (stop-loss)

The 'limited risk protection' facility allows you to trade CFDs while limiting your losses to an agreed and guaranteed maximum. When you trade on a limited risk basis you specify a stop-loss level at which you are guaranteed to be closed out, should the market move sharply against you.

You have to pay extra to take out a stop-loss – think of it as an insurance premium. Typically this in the region of 0.3% of the value of the transaction and is in addition to normal commission charges. Not all CFD providers offer this facility and terms vary so it is wise to check before opening an account.

Here's how the guaranteed stop-loss works in practice:

Using stop-loss when buying Kingfisher

Opening the position

Kingfisher is quoted at 212.5/213p in the market and you buy 5,000 shares as a CFD at 213p, the offer price.

You decide to set your guaranteed stop-loss at 190p. That means that if the market moves against you, your position will be closed at exactly 190p, even if, for example, the share opened at a substantially lower level following an overnight profits warning.

The most you can lose on the position (excluding interest and dividend adjustments) is £1,150:

213p, the opening level, minus 190p, the stop level = 23p

23p × 5,000 shares = £1,150

The transaction commission is 0.25% or £27 (5,000 shares × 213p × 0.25%).

The limited risk (stop-loss) premium is also charged when you open the position. In this case it is 0.3% or £32 (5,000 shares × 213p × 0.3%).

Interest and dividend adjustments

Interest and dividend adjustments are applied to limited risk positions in exactly the same way as to standard CFD positions.

Triggering the guaranteed stop-loss

Suppose that you hold the position for a few weeks without much happening. Then suddenly one morning the whole sector opens sharply lower after negative overnight news. Kingfisher closed the previous day at 195p, but it opens at 180p. Your guaranteed stop-loss is triggered and your position is closed at 190p even though the share opened well below this level. Your 5,000 shares are sold at 190p. The commission on the transaction is 0.25% or £24 (5000 shares × 190p × 0.25%)

Your loss on the trade is calculated as follows:

Opening level	213p
Closing level	190p
Difference	23p
Loss on trade:	23p × 5,000 shares = £1,150

Without the guaranteed stop-loss you would have been lucky to close your position at 180p, representing a loss on the position of over £1,500.

Calculating the overall result

To calculate the overall result of the transaction you also have to take account of the commission and limited risk premium you have paid, together with any interest and dividend adjustments. In this example you might have held the position open for 30 days, at a total interest cost of say, £56. Assume there are no dividends.

Your total loss is calculated as follows:

Loss on trade	(£1,150)
Commission	(£51)
Limited risk premium	(£32)

Using the guaranteed stop-loss

When you buy a share or any other financial security in the normal way, you do so in the expectation that price will increase, but you have no protection if it goes down. In theory you stand to lose 100% of your investment.

When you trade CFDs, on the other hand, you can limit your potential losses at the outset of each trade to a figure you are comfortable with by using the guaranteed stop-loss.

I love it! It's totally brilliant! At a typical cost of £30 per £10,000, stop-loss is an absolute bargain.

Some trading strategies make stop-loss too expensive. For instance, if you are a day-trader running positions for only a few hours or minutes, then the additional cost of the limited risk premium is likely to outweigh the advantages.

However, if your horizons are days, weeks or months then you will probably find it worthwhile to use the guaranteed stop-loss strategically. You don't need to put a stop-loss willy-nilly on every position you open. There is no point in paying for something you do not need and stop-losses can on occasion work against you – suppose Kingfisher, in the example above, had shot back up again after you had been stopped out.

Consider each trade on its own merits before deciding whether to set a stop-loss.

Here are a few tips about using stop-loss that I have learned the hard way:

Setting the limit

There are no hard and fast rules on this but as a general rule I think it is a mistake to set the limit too near to the opening price of your trade. In other words, if you buy at 190p and set the stop-loss at 185p, there is a danger that a minor negative movement will close you out just before the price shoots up.

So how near to your opening price should you set your stop-loss? This will depend on the risk you are prepared to take and the volatility of both the share you are trading and that of the market as a whole.

As the share price moves, you can move the point where you set the stop-loss.

This is important because if, say, the share price doubles, you might want to raise the stop-loss point to protect some of your

Volatility

Volatility simply means how fast a price moves up and down. If a share price of a stock moves up and down rapidly over a short time period, it is said to have high volatility, and if the price almost never changes, it is said to have low volatility.

High volatility tends to be associated with riskier shares, such as small firms, fast-growing companies, the high tech sector and overvalued shares that have very high p/es.

Although traditionally regarded with concern, high volatility is not necessarily a bad thing, especially if you are a short-term trader, since you can make a profit quickly as the share price bounces up and down.

profits. Thus, in the example above, if Kingfisher had gone up to,say, 240p then by moving the stop-loss up to, say, 216p, you preserve the gain, eliminate the possibility of making a loss on the trade and are on for a free ride if the share price keeps on rising.

Stop-loss in long positions

The stock market is a mysterious beast and events outside our control, the timing of which it is impossible to predict, can wreak havoc. A war, a major bankruptcy, a political scandal or any one of countless possibilities may suddenly cause the market to drop – a one day loss of 25% is perfectly feasible.

This kind of sudden drop may not matter to the long term investor, but for short term traders like us it can be a nightmare. I tend to use the stop-loss to a greater extent when holding long (buy) positions, than I do when holding short (sell) positions. This is because while the market may fall by 25% in a day, it is not likely to suddenly rise by 25% in a day.

Another reason why you need stop-loss is the profits warning. This is when a company is forced by the regulations to announce that its profits for a given period are likely to be less than previously estimated. Issuing a warning is typically followed by an instant fall in the share price of 20–40%.

Using the stop-loss will protect you from this, but what were you doing going long on a company where there was the remotest possibility of a profits warning? That doesn't say much for your judgement!

Stop-loss: short positions

The whole market may be unlikely to go up by 25% in a day, but one company's share price may do so. If another firm announces that it is bidding to purchase the company, the share price could instantly shoot up by as much as 40%.

If you are short, that means an instant loss for you. For this reason, when you short it is important to assess the likelihood of this happening.

It does happen quite a lot because companies in trouble with falling share prices attract predators.

You don't only go short on companies that are in trouble – often you may go short on ones that are very successful – but not *that* successful. In other words, it's not the company that has a problem it's the share price, i.e. it's too high, in your opinion.

Stop-loss: win–win

I don't want to kill the goose that lays the golden eggs by publicizing another little stop-loss wrinkle, so I'll only give you a few hints and you can try to work it out for yourself. I wouldn't have seen it in a million years, but my son James saw it in a flash. We were in the pub at the time and he sketched it out on a beer mat. The next day I was all set to use it when the markets opened.

So here's a hint; it has to do with takeovers and profit warnings. Look for companies where there's a pretty good chance that sooner or later one or the other is going to happen; companies where there's say, a 50:50 chance of a 40% gain. Make a list of all the ones you can find. Ring up your CFD provider and see if they'll let you do the trades. It's a can't lose proposition, so they may refuse you.

That's all I'm going to say about it. James thinks we should share it. He is thinking about running a competition or posting it on the internet. Well, he discovered it, so he is entitled to do so – but I'm not breathing another word!

Chapter 7

Spread betting

As we saw in Chapter 5, one of the attractions of CFDs is that that they are not subject to stamp duty. This can amount to a very substantial saving if you trade frequently. CFDs aren't entirely free of tax, though – you will still have to pay capital gains tax (CGT) on profits over and above any losses and your annual allowance, just as you would on normal share trading.

With spread betting, on the other hand, any gains you make are entirely free of CGT. That's because the government regards spread betting as out-and-out gambling, and they don't tax gambling profits – yet. If spread betting became so popular that too many people were making too much money, the government might easily change the tax rules, but for now they are CGT-free. Remember, though, that since you don't have to pay tax on the profits from spread betting, you can't set any losses against your CGT bill either.

In general, spread bets and CFDs are very similar but there are some other differences you should now about:

- Spread bets are less flexible than CFDs because they have set expiry dates, while you can close a CFD at any time.

- The bid–offer spread on a CFD is usually narrower than the spread on an equivalent spread bet – so it's cheaper for you.

What is a 'spread'?

The spread is the difference between the selling and buying price set by the spread betting firm in any given market, for example 108–110. If you believe a price will rise, it means you will take a long position and buy at 110; if you believe the price will fall, you will go short and sell at the lower price of 108.

- You don't pay transaction commissions when you spread bet, but you do on CFDs – but as we saw in the last chapter, the CFD commissions are pretty low at around 0.25%.

- When you are long, your CFD position attracts an interest charge, calculated daily. Spread bets are free of this.

How spread betting works

The spread price from a spread betting firm will differ slightly from the underlying price (or index, currency or whatever else you are betting on). This is because all charges, costs and the profit margin for the spread betting firm are included in the spread. Moreover, factors such as the interest cost of trading on margin, and any dividends due over the life of the bet will also influence the price. This also means that, apart from the spread, there are no further charges levied on the bet.

Spread betting is well suited to short-term and medium-traders, offering daily and weekly contracts, together with the opportunity to hold your position for as long as six months. Spread betting positions can be opened or closed at any time during the life of your bet; if you forget, it will be automatically closed on the relevant expiry date.

When you ask for a quote from a spread betting firm you do not have to let them know straight away whether you are buying or selling. Once the quote is given, and you are happy with the price, you then say whether you want to buy or sell and for how much a point. The advent of internet trading means that you can trade via your laptop computer from anywhere in the world, with either a telephone or modem.

Example: going long on Vodafone

It is January and Vodafone shares are trading at 120p. You feel that the price of Vodafone will rise at some time between now and March. The spread betting price for March Vodafone is 121–122.

You decide to 'buy' March Vodafone for, say, £10 per penny movement in the share price – equivalent to buying 1,000 under-lying shares – and you do this at the higher end of the spread, 122p.

Rather than putting up the full value of the purchase as you would with a stockbroker (£1,220), you leave an initial margin (deposit, in plain English) in your account with the spread betting firm, typ-ically 10% of the underlying share value, or £122 in this case.

Let's say that you are correct in your view and the shares go up to 134p. You decide to close the bet and take your profit. You ask for a price on March Vodafone and are quoted 135–136.

You sell £10 at the lower end of the spread at 135p.

Your tax free profit is:

£130, i.e. (135 – 122 × £10)

on a margin deposit of £122.

There are no other charges or commissions to pay.

Using stop-losses

To minimize the impact of a trade going against you, it is sensible to place stop-losses - specifying a price at which the trade should be closed if it is going the wrong way. With most spread betting firms there is no charge for this, but in very fast moving markets, your stop-loss might not be triggered at the level you requested. A guaranteed stop-loss, however, does offer complete protection at your chosen stop-loss level and involves a small charge.

So no matter what happens in the markets you can have absolute peace of mind. Spread betting may sound complicated at first, but it can be learned quickly. Many firms have test sites or trading simulators where you can practise your technique with "virtual money". One way of learning 'live' but with minimal risk is to open an account with Finspreads and take advantage of its Trading Academy which lets you trade at just 1p a point - real money – for the first eight weeks.

Remember that there are two types of stop-loss. The guaranteed stop-loss assures you that you will be closed at the price you have set, and there is a charge. The ordinary stop-loss is free but

Example: using the stop-loss

Suppose you are bullish on the Square Cannonball Company which is currently at 100p. Your spread betting firm quotes you a spread of 99–101p.

You decide to bet £5 a point that the share price will rise. This means that for every penny that the price rises above 101p you will make a profit of £5. It's the equivalent of buying 500 shares at 100p.

Your spread betting company asks you for a 10% margin payment, which is, say, 10% of this amount: £50.

After a few weeks the Square Cannonball Company's share price begins to fall. Your spread betting company now quotes 79–81p. You decide to cut your losses:

Initial bet:	£5 a point
Price opened:	101p
Price closed:	79p
Difference:	−22
Loss at £5 a point:	22 × £5 = £110

£110 is more than the £50 you put up as a margin deposit, so your firm would have asked you for more cash as the price fell.

Suppose you had set a guaranteed stop-loss at the outset at 90p. As soon as the price had fallen to 90p, you would have been closed out, making an 11 point loss of £55.

you take the risk that if the share price moves very sharply against you, you may not be able to close at the stop-loss price, in which case you stand to lose much more than you had anticipated.

Compare the firms

For the past few years stock markets around the world have been falling and there as been a huge increase in interest in CFDs and spread betting. These two facts are not unrelated! Perhaps the main attraction has been the ability to go short, but it also suggests that many people are using derivatives for the first time – they can't all be shrewd investors, so be cautious about the opinions people offer and compare the services offered by the different brokers carefully.

In the UK, the main firms offering these facilities are:

- Cannon Bridge Corporation

- Cantor Index CFDs

- City Markets

- Deal4free.com

- GNI Touch

- Halewood International

- IFX Limited

- IG Markets

- Kyte Clients

- Man Financial

- Saxo Bank

- Sucden Equity CFDs

Most of these firms offer user-friendly websites and the ability to trade online. That's all very nice and consumer-orientated, but obviously they are encouraging you to bet, so don't get too carried away by the company research materials they offer. It's essential to think for yourself and only make trades when you are personally sure of what you are doing.

At any one time, the various firms may offer very different spreads on the same share, so it pays to compare them. The bigger the spread, the more you are paying the firm.

Do your own research

In the next two chapters we will look at how to find trading opportunities. If you have been a stock market investor for some time, you probably have a feel for certain companies and sectors in the market. Build on your knowledge! The great mistake is to get excited about something you don't really know much about – say the Hang Seng index in Hong Kong – and get unduly influenced by someone else's opinions or a good story in the press. That's fatal. Veteran traders don't listen to other people's views, except to note what is fashionable. Especially when you are shorting, you are essentially contradicting everyone else's opinion in the market, so you'll be on your own. Successful trading is most definitely not a group activity!

Chapter 8

Spotting the trading opportunities

So now you've got the tools and you have a basic idea of how to use them. The next question is: where do you find the money-making situations? You are looking for companies that are either potentially big winners or potentially big losers, which I call the 'money-makers' – they may not be making money for themselves, but they will for me.

Other people may be content with small profits but if you follow my method the situation shouldn't merely be 'attractive', it must be drop-dead gorgeous, or it isn't worth the effort. I want to achieve high returns from trading. If all I can do is a fraction more than the average return on a long-term investment, which is about 4% a year, adjusted for inflation, then it isn't worth the effort.

Tuning in

Fortunately, good opportunities are all around you. You have to attune yourself to the 'money-makers'. They are staring you in the face. It's just a matter of seeing that they are there.

The kind of companies I'm talking about are consumer businesses selling to the mass market. Consumers are people like you and me. Consumers decide which stores and products they are going to favour and which ones they are going to stay away from. As a group, consumers have enormous power and as individuals consumers have an understanding of why they buy some things and not others. You don't need a bunch of stock market analysts to tell you why a good consumer business is successful – you can go and see for yourself. Forget the clever numbers and the deliberate mystification of finance! Ignore all those brokers and advisers who claim to know better than you! Get out of your armchair and go shopping!

Go to the high streets and the shopping malls and see what is actually happening to the stores and products. Which ones are generating excitement? Which ones aren't working? You don't have to wait for the accounts to be published – you'll see what is going on as it happens.

You're going to go long on the winners and short the losers, so you're interested in both extremes. Which shops are empty? Which ones are packed? Ask shoppers what they think about the place. Do the same with pubs, restaurants, hotels, leisure centres, sports centres and health clubs. Try them out for yourself and see which ones you like.

Talk to the staff who work there. If you have a few casual chats, you'll know the score. You can pretend to be a bit stupid, or to have verbal diarrhoea. Ask questions like, "Always this busy, is it?" or "Always this quiet, is it?" They'll give you an answer – most of them are bored and don't have much loyalty. You can probe quite deeply sometimes:

"And why's that? The new range? People don't like it? What, they love it? And how often does it change? Every two weeks? And that's good, is it? It has been since they got a new designer in? How long ago was that? Six months? And it's been like this ever since? The turnover must be going through the roof. It has tripled? Someone must be doing alright! Better than alright? How come? They're getting it all made in China now? And that's good, is it? Twice as good? Better quality, half the price? Half the price, twice the profit? Wow! Three times the turnover, twice the profit . . ."

Philip Fisher and 'scuttlebutt'

Philip Fisher was a highly successful American investor who began his career in the 1930s during the Depression. Reputed to be 'remorselessly thorough', Fisher made a fortune over his long life by researching companies very deeply before he invested and holding for the very long term.

One of Fisher's main techniques was what he called 'scuttlebutt' or 'the business grapevine'. He would talk to the employees, ex-employees, customers and competitors of the firm he was interested in and attended trade shows to chat to salespeople about their industry. In his book *Common Stocks and Uncommon Profits*, he writes that 'the business grapevine is a remarkable thing . . . most people, particularly if they feel sure there is no danger of their being quoted, like to talk about the field of work in which they are engaged, and will talk rather freely about their competition. Go to five companies in an industry, ask each of them intelligent questions about the points of strength and weakness of the other four, and nine times out of ten a surprisingly detailed and accurate picture of all five will emerge.'

Don't feel that you're wasting your time wandering around shopping malls. Tell yourself that you are shopping for profit, instead of spending money on throw-away goods. Everyone else is spending, but you'll be making money once you have spotted the right money-making situation. You have to get yourself into a new habit, a new way of seeing. After a while it becomes a way of life. It will be the first thing that you look for: is this company a potential winner or loser?

Always look in to the situation as deeply as possible. If you see a busy shop, you need to find out why it's busy. There may be all kinds of reasons – for instance, that it's raining and there is nowhere else to go. You have to do your homework, visit more outlets and go at different times of the day.

The next question is, have others seen it? Is the news already there in the share price? Is your priceless insight merely old news?

Chapter 9

Analysing companies

So you think you have spotted a winner or a loser. Now you have to check it out more closely. If everyone else has spotted it too, the share price will already have moved. To make a profit, you need to find the ones that other people have missed.

The first thing to check is if the company is quoted on the stock exchange. If it is not, you have virtually no chance of buying the shares, so all you can do is keep an eye on it and wait to see if it ever comes to market.

If it is quoted, the next step is to examine the published information. Let's take Hennes as an example – this was a highly successful retail chain that I came to quite late and decided not to touch, but it shows how I approach the job of analysis.

Researching Hennes

Not all quoted companies are household names. When my daughter started raving about a shop called Hennes I had no idea what she was talking about. She took me along to see – the place looked as if a bomb had hit, with hordes of teenage girls spending like maniacs.

When I got home, I looked up Hennes on the *Financial Times* website, FT.com. It costs £5 a month for the basic membership, which gives you almost all of the information I need to research listed firms. You can pay more for deeper levels of analysis, but I'm an 'Alanist', not an 'analyst', and I don't like to get too bogged down in detail.

I typed in 'Hennes' and discovered that they were the largest fashion retailer in Europe. Hennes and Mauritz, a Swedish firm, were mega trendy and mega successful.

The FT website lets you search for all *Financial Times* articles mentioning your chosen key words. I searched for articles on Hennes:

Lex Column
Hennes & Mauritz
Financial Times, 23 March 2002

As Europe's top fashion retailers strutted along the earnings catwalk this week, H&M almost upstaged the sparkling display of rivals Inditex and Next. First quarter profits, up 100%, beat all forecasts. Strong sales growth helped, but the biggest factor was a 7 percentage point increase in the gross margin to a record 52.9% as tighter buying reduced the level of markdowns.

This, of course, is what the Swedish retailer was aiming for. A few seasons of poor inventory management had left it discounting and running the risk that customers would stop buying at full price in expectation of another sale soon. Hence the shift in emphasis from top line growth and store openings to operational improvements and raising margins. Attempting to revamp its supply chain, reducing lead times for products and rotating them more frequently, should bring it closer to the industry-leading model of Inditex's Zara chain. It should also reduce the perennial fashion retailer's risk: getting saddled with too many goods that nobody wants to buy.

But H&M's first-quarter margin in 2001 was exceptionally poor after heavy discounting; the underlying improvement was less dramatic. And there were warning bells. US sales increased only 10% in dollar terms, though H&M had triple the number of stores –casting further doubt on what was supposed to be one of its biggest growth markets. At over 30 times forward earnings. H&M still vies with Inditex to be Europe's most highly-rated retailer. If Inditex looks expensive enough, H&M looks overpriced.

If you want more detailed information then you can use your FT.com password to access the Investor's Chronicle website at a reasonably small annual fee. This gives you the 'Chronic''s interpretation of the company's results along with broker recommendations and other information. Personally, I don't find it necessary. I like to make my own mind up.

When I read the material on Hennes I knew that at 30 times earnings I wasn't going to make a killing on it. Even though it was expensive I didn't think it was worth betting against it.

I decided to look at its share price history anyway to see if I had missed anything.

Share price history

On the FT website you select 'markets data and tools', enter the name or reference number of the share and you'll get a graph of the share price together with the current share price. Then you click 'analytical charting', re-enter the name/code and you are given a more detailed share price chart which allows you to adjust the time scale from one day to 'All Data'.

Figure 9.1 shows the Hennes 'All Data' chart. From this you can see that either they floated at the end of 1998 or that the chart provider (BigCharts.Com) has no earlier information. If I need to know if they floated at the end of 1998 I can discover this by going back to the relevant FT.com articles. In this case there was no need to do so because all the action took place in 1999/2000. Since then the price had been moving in the 180–200 kr range. From what I had seen in the store they were doing well, but at 30 times earnings the news was already in the share price. If the market rose they might rise with it but in the long term I'd expect Hennes to fall. There wasn't enough in it either way to make it an attractive situation.

Figure 9.1 Hennes 1999–2003

Valuing the business

When you have established that the company is quoted on the stock market, brought yourself up to date on the story so far and examined the history of the share price, it's a good idea to print out the share price graph. Comparing the graph with the news stories, you should be able to relate how various events have affected the market value of the company. Total time expended on research: about half an hour.

Hennes was not what I was looking for. It was overvalued, but not overvalued enough for me to be licking my lips and deciding to sell it short. What I'm looking for is a situation where there is a very serious discrepancy between what I have seen on the ground and the valuation that the market has given the business – which is implied by its share price. In order to know if it is a serious discrepancy, I have to give the company a 'realistic' valuation, which is a very subjective judgement to make.

There are many ways to value a company. A conventional analyst would undertake a lot of very time-consuming and thorough work, examining the profit and loss account, balance sheet, cash flow statement, accountant's notes and so on. I'm an 'Alanist' not an analyst and I don't do that – that's what I had a Finance Director for.

If you want to learn how the conventional analysts do it, there are endless textbooks and handbooks that will tell you. As far as I'm concerned, life's too short. I'm just not clever enough to do it – but that doesn't mean I can't make money by using my judgement.

How to be an 'Alanist'

As an 'Alanist', I still take financial information seriously. Once I have familiarized myself with the big picture, I want to know what the analysts – you know, the smart arses with the calculators – are thinking. FT.com gives me a bunch of analyst reports if I want to read them. They may be completely worng – and believe me, they often are – but it is important to know what they are saying, especially if you are thinking of betting in the opposite direction. For instance, if the analysts are all saying a company is a 'Strong Buy' and you are thinking of going short, you need to be as sure as you can be that they are wrong and you are right because their employers' sales force will be pushing their recommended shares at all and sundry. If you are betting against the herd you had better be right.

I have two main questions:

1. What is the current market capitalization?

2. How much are the profits likely to be?

Divide (1) by (2) and you have the price/earning (p/e) multiple. It is pretty well the only measure I use. I can understand it, so can you, and so can anyone else. Discounted cashflow may be a more sophisticated and profound measure, but I can't follow it. Tell me the profits and the market capitalization and I know whether I'm interested. What interests me are very high and very low p/es in relation to:

•   The market as a whole

•   The relevant sector of the market

- Plain common sense

Over the long term the average p/e of companies quoted on the London stock exchange has been around 13 or 14. In the bear market trough of 1974 when the lights literally did go out (because of the power cuts), the average p/e fell to 5. At its peak in 1999, the average p/e was over 30. At the time of writing it is about 16, on the high side but not drastically so.

What really matters is the p/e of the company in relation to the market average. At the height of the dotcom boom there were high-tech firms that had no earnings, and thus no p/e, and some that had p/es in the 100s, while old-fashioned firms were on p/es of 4 or 5. It was the kind of market madness that offers opportunities for people who can think for themselves.

Most analysts will tell you to compare the company p/e with its sector average p/e as well as to the market. It has always been a mystery to me how sectors go in and out of fashion. Why should the telecom and media sectors be trading on an average p/e that is 10 times the p/e of housebuilders? I don't know the answer, but as a trader what's more important is whether the company p/e is way out of line with its sector's. If it is, then if I'm right I'll make a large profit.

A rule of thumb

At current interest rates (say 3%), I would not want to go long on a company with a p/e over 15. If it is higher than that, I'm much more likely to sell it short. If I think I have found a winner and I'm going to go long, I'll want the p/e to be under 10.

The best opportunities to short are often those companies that have made no profits and therefore have no p/e at all, or have only just started making profits and have a very high p/e, say over 30, although it depends on the sector.

Second impressions

So you have found what looks like a winner. You have seen the company's operations with your own eyes and by any standards it is on a low p/e. Or you have found a loser – you know that it is not doing well because you have seen for yourself, but it is trading on a high p/e. In either situation, the word has not yet got out to the market.

If you are going to risk a lot of money, go back and visit other parts of the company's operations. If it is a retailer, go to more stores in different areas. I'll bet my impressions on the ground against any analyst's recommendation, however clever they are.

Don't bet against the market

Perhaps 'try not to bet against the market' is more realistic advice. If you are long in a falling market or short in a rising market you may have a very long wait before you are proved right. Often you don't know if the market is rising or falling, which makes life more difficult. At the time of writing the market has been falling for three years, so it's been a shorter's paradise. The easy money has been in shorting internet stocks and the like. That's not to say that there haven't been any good opportunities to go long, it's just that you had to be very sure indeed that the firm was a winner.

Sometimes some sectors are on an up trend while other sectors are falling out of bed – for example, in the dotcom boom, 'old economy' shares headed south, and then reversed as the tech stocks crashed.

In the following chapters we'll look at how the 'Alanist' approach has worked for me in practice in specific cases. I hope you enjoy them – I certainly enjoy the actual process of speculation, especially when I come out on top. If I were to offer on basic piece of advice for this kind of trading, it would be:

Stick to what you know

It's easy to believe good stories about businesses you don't know very much about – the grass is always greener. It's harder to fool yourself about something you really understand, which is why, when those good opportunities occasionally turn up, you'll know them for what they are and be able to act.

Chapter 10

Eidos

I fell for Lara more than thirty years ago. It was 1965 and Julie Christie was playing her in *Dr Zhivago*, David Lean's epic Oscar-winning movie. Lara was so flawless and Yuri Zhivago's love for her so tragic that her image has stayed with me ever since. Most men have a perfect ideal of a woman tucked away somewhere in a secret corner of their souls. Lara was mine; even her name bewitched me.

Suddenly in the nineties I started hearing her name again: Lara, the busty animated hero of some bizarre computer game called Tomb Raider. I was privately outraged. Was nothing sacred? The computer geeks told me I didn't understand. I didn't want to understand.

"You should see her body," said the geeks. It all sounded very sad, but my business instincts were tickled. If a lot of grown men thought Lara was great and were prepared to spend money on her, there had to be a reason. "Go on, tell me all about her," I said to the geeks. And they did, but they were even more excited about the next generation machine, Playstation 2, than they were about Lara.

The geeks were losing me. Next generation? Playstation 2? Something you play with? Here were a bunch of young men who never left their rooms because they were 'playing' with an animated girl on their TV screens.

I took my eight-year-old into a games shop and found a copy of Tomb Raider with Lara on the cover. It looked about right for his older brother. I took it to the counter and started talking to the staff. They couldn't believe that I was so naïve that I didn't know about Lara. They thought I was from another planet. They were right. I was from Planet Earth, and they were on Planet Eidos.

Eidos was the company that made Tomb Raider and some other games. I looked it up when I got home. It was based in the UK. The good news was that its shares were listed but the share price wasn't going anywhere, even though the firm was selling millions of pounds' worth of copies of Tomb Raider.

I dug a little deeper to find out what was keeping the shares grounded and the penny eventually dropped. Creative types had control of the company. When that happens it doesn't matter how much money the firm is making, because they'll find a way to spend it. I had some experience of this because the television company HTV had had a similar problem a few years back and I'd been invited to join the board to help bring them back down to earth.

Eidos came down to earth when Coopers & Lybrand, their auditors, announced their resignation in mid-1997, apparently because they were unhappy with the way things were being run. It wasn't a big surprise; the annual reports for the last two financial years stated that the company had not followed the Cadbury Report's guidelines for corporate governance. Eidos had grown incredibly fast, mainly by acquisitions and investing in worldwide licensing deals, and had been listed on the NASDAQ market

The Cadbury Report

Companies that are listed on the stock market are very highly regulated, but some firms cut corners, particularly during boom times when everyone seems to be making money. When the crash comes, firms that have broken the rules are called to account, regulations are revised and there is a big drive to improve 'corporate governance' (the way companies are administered). Then another boom comes along and it starts all over again.

In 1991 the tycoon Robert Maxwell died in mysterious circumstances just before it was discovered that he had stolen an estimated £500,000 from the pension funds of the Mirror Group of newspapers. Shortly before this, a massive international bank, BCCI, had collapsed leaving its depositors high and dry, and the textile-to-fruit giant Polly Peck went bust, with its boss, Asil Nadir, fleeing to Northern Cyprus to avoid extradition.

They were juicy scandals of a kind that is familiar to experienced investors, but caused terrible damage to the lives of thousands of employees, customers and investors who had trusted the authorities to make sure that large firms are run honestly.

The government's response was to commission the Cadbury Report, which set out a code of conduct for listed companies. The Code has been much imitated by regulators in other countries and is intended, among other things, to prevent a single individual to gain so much control of the daily management of a firm that he or she can break the law with impunity. It also encourages companies to produce truthful and open accounts. Although it is not a perfect guarantee, adherence to the Cadbury Code is a hopeful sign that a company is being run honestly.

in the US, which meant they had a whole new set of US rules to follow as well as the British ones.

The share price dropped by half and I started paying close attention. Eidos promised to get itself in order and off it went again. The shares doubled again. Then they halved again. I decided to tuck a few shares away when they were at £6 and the price/earnings ratio was nice and low after a market drop. This company was selling millions of games and earning serious money, remember, so the p/e really meant something, unlike some of the dot-com fantasies of the time.

The price moved up from £6 to £7. The highest it had ever been was £12.62 and I thought it could get back there. I could easily see it reaching £14 if the market held up. If the market crashed again, they might drop to £5. I decided to buy 1500 shares at £7 – that's risking £10,500, and putting up a £1050 margin. I decided that if the price dropped to £5 I would buy another 1,500 shares which would put me at a further risk of £7,500, so my total risk would be £18,000. If the price went up to £12, I would sell for £36,000, doubling my money. If the price went down to £4, I would lose £6,000, but if the price went that low, someone might bid for the company.

Compared with the market average p/e of 24, Eidos was on a low valuation – if its price went up as high as £14 per share, its p/e would still only be 12. My feeling was the company should be trading at a premium to the market, not at a discount. Eidos was actually making a profit which was more than many of the highly valued tech stocks that had yet to earn any money at all.

By the autumn of 1998, the market was 'going gangbusters', as Sir John Harvey-Jones says. Eidos' share price was up, Tomb Raider 3 was due out and Christmas was coming:

Tomb Raider helps Eidos advance

(*Financial Times*, 20 January 1999)

The popularity of Lara Croft, heroine of the Tomb Raider series, remained undiminished over the Christmas period, helping Eidos, the computer games group, to report a rise in quarterly sales. As a result, operating profits for the year to March 31, would be "substantially in excess of current market expectations", Eidos said. The shares rose 65p to £11.65. Eidos launched the third-generation of the game, Tomb Raider 3, in time for the Christmas buying season. The title, which appeals in particular to teenage boys, was well received by the computer games industry. The company said it shipped an estimated 6m units of its games in the three months to December 31. This included other successful titles such as Ninja, Michael Owen's World League Soccer, Gangsters and The Unholy War. It was a similar story a year ago, when the success of Tomb Raider 2 over Christmas again lifted Eidos shares and led to a raft of profit upgrades. Yesterday, analysts raised their annual profit forecasts from £30m to £35m before exceptional items and goodwill. Last year, the company made profits of £16.5m on sales of £137m.

I was in the money and hoping for more. By February 1999, Eidos was at £15:

Eidos boosted by Lara Croft

(*Financial Times*, 26 February 1999)

The continuing popularity of Lara Croft, the heroine of the

Tomb Raider computer game series, helped Eidos, one of Europe's largest developers and publishers of games software, report better than expected third-quarter results yesterday.

Tomb Raider III, the latest version of the game, was launched in November and, together with six other titles which achieved sales in excess of 350,000 units, helped boost profits in the crucial third quarter by 64 per cent to £51.3m (£31.3m).

Pre-tax profits for the nine months to December 31 rose to £32.4m (£13m) as the group began to realise the benefits of its expanded portfolio of titles, which included 13 titles launched during the period.

It just got better and better. By March Eidos was at £20. In May the results came out:

Games popularity buoys Eidos

(*Financial Times*, 28 May 1999)

The growing popularity of computer games helped Eidos, the developer of hit titles such as Tomb Raider and Championship Manager, more than double annual pre-tax profits to £37.9m. The figure, an increase from £16.5m the previous year, was struck on revenues 65 per cent higher at £226.3m.

Tomb Raider III, the third in the series starring Lara Croft, sold more than 4m copies in the year to March. Its continuing success has prompted Paramount, the entertainment group, to turn the game into a film later this year from which Eidos will receive royalties. Charles Cornwall, chief executive, said a director had been contracted, although the role of Lara Croft had not yet been cast. Demi Moore, Sharon Stone and Catherine Zeta Jones had all been mooted for the role, he said.

However, Mr Cornwall emphasised the success of the group's other titles. Commando, Championship Manager and several other games had all sold more than 350,000 copies during the past year. "Our revenues have come from a broad portfolio of titles," he said.

Publishing deals with Free Radical Design and Michael Crichton's Timeline Studios would yield further launches this year, in addition to Eidos's own stable of releases.

Earnings per share increased from 64.1p to 141.5p. There is again no dividend.

Comment

Eidos has been fighting more battles than some of the characters in its games. One has been to lay the ghost of the stock's previously erratic history when it was buffeted by unfounded rumours of insider dealing. Another has been to establish the credibility of the management in what is perceived as a notoriously volatile industry. And while Tomb Raider has been the group's pot of gold, it has also become the product that defines Eidos. Critics wonder how well the group could whether a decline in Lara's fortunes. Yesterday's results answered all these questions admirably. The strong performance across a range of titles, the signing and strengthening of industry alliances and close attention to the cost base indicate a well focused management. In addition to the slate of new titles to be launched this year, Eidos is developing an internet games portal that could prove its biggest success yet. Pre-tax profit forecasts for this year of £54m, put the shares on a forward p/e of 10.8. A buying opportunity.

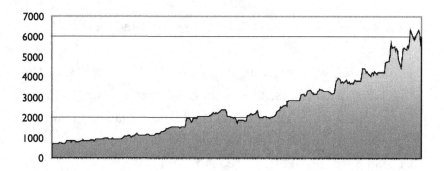

Figure 10.1 Eidos Oct. 1998–Dec. 1999

The price dropped back a bit during the run up to the annual results. On the day of the announcement the shares were at £18. Three months later they were at £33, and three months after that £63.

According to the press they were still a buy, even at this level. I sold out – and was very tempted to short. Eidos made a 5 for 1 scrip issue because at £60 a share, the high price might be putting investors off.

Scrip issue – also called a 'bonus issue' or a 'capitalization issue', this is the issue of additional shares by a company to its shareholders in proportion to their holdings. The effect is simply to increase the number of shares in the company, which also reduces the share price – for instance, if the share price is £60 and the company doubles the number of shares through a scrip issue, the share price will be £30 and the existing shareholders will have twice as many shares as they did before, although their total holding will have the same value.

There is no cost to the shareholders. Companies often do this when their share price has risen substantially, on the grounds that new investors may shy away from a high-priced share. When looking at share price charts, you will often see that they have been adjusted for scrip issues (see Figure 10.2) which changes the pre-scrip issue prices from what they actually were at the time to what they were in relation to the post-scrip issue prices.

Volume – volume is simply the number of shares that actually changed hands during a given time period. It is useful to study volume because it tells you something about the 'popularity' of a share at a particular time.

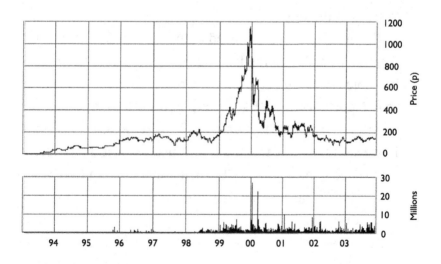

Figure 10.2 Eidos adjusted for 5 for 1 scrip issue

Here's what the *FT* was saying about them at the end of the year:

Lara Croft turns respectable and wins City friends: Eidos, her creator, is close to matching her popularity

(*Financial Times*, 16 December 1999)

Not even Lara Croft, the improbably endowed heroine of Tomb Raider, has seen as much action this year as the shares of Eidos, the computer game's developer. This week they hit a new high, as the company unveiled a deal with the Disney entertainment group to develop three new computer games

It left the shares celebrating an 11-fold gain over the past 12 months, and outperforming the FT All-Share index five-fold on the way. Indeed, not even last month's increased half-year losses and lower revenues could stem investor appetite. The rise is all the more remarkable because of both the nature of Eidos's business and its previously poor relations with the City.

The group has become used to the perception that it is too dependent on Tomb Raider. The game's massive success - it has sold some 5m copies in its various versions - has meant that Eidos's fortunes have ridden on how each sequel has been received by critics and public alike. Against the odds, however, Eidos has sustained the success of Tomb Raider in a crowded games market. It is being made into a Hollywood film, which suggests that its longevity will be guaranteed for some time yet.

At the same time, Eidos's success in nourishing other best-sellers has also been recognised. Championship Manager and Formula One, for example, are two of half a dozen titles that have achieved sales of more than 1m. This has resulted in the Tomb Raider franchise accounting for an increasingly smaller proportion of group revenues. In the past three years, it has shrunk from 90 to 57 per cent. Next year, analysts are forecasting, it could fall to as low as 30 per cent of group sales.

Another crucial factor in Eidos's growing popularity with investors is its improved relations with the City. Two years ago, erratic movements in the share price added to market concerns over the quality of the business and fortitude of the management. In addition, Charles Cornwall, chief executive, had a low profile, as did other senior executives.

However, much has changed in the past 18 months. The directors and company advisers have undertaken a charm offensive with large institutional investors, leading to Eidos's share register now including many of the big names in fund management.

The management's reputation has also been helped by corporate activity in the past year, which has seen investments in a range of smaller games studios, in Europe and the US, underlining the group's determination to widen its portfolio. Deals, such as that truck with Disney this week, have underpinned this trend.

The result of all this has been the significant re-rating of the stock.

Helen Snell at ABN Amro says that Eidos's perception a year ago had led to the stock trading on a p/e below nine. "It was grossly underrated," she says. Now, however, with the surge in the past year, the stock is trading on a forward multiple of 30. "Even that is not expensive, when compared with competitors such as Electronic Arts in the US, which trades on 40-plus," says Ms Snell. "And Eidos has a better earnings record and a diversified portfolio of titles."

A month later the party was over – the price had dropped to £25:

Eidos shares fall by a third after profits warning
(*Financial Times*, 19 January 2000)

Shares in Eidos, one of the star performing stocks of 1999, crashed by a third yesterday after the computer games developer warned profits would be hit by poor Christmas sales. The fall, by £12.60 to £26.28, undermines the management's efforts to repair relations with investors over the past 18 months.

The company has been attempting to quell the share price volatility it was previously renowned for. It has also been trying to recast itself as a multi-faceted developer, increasingly less reliant on its main blockbuster title Tomb Raider. Indeed, the latest version of the best-selling game, which stars the buxom heroine Lara Croft, was one of the few bright spots in an otherwise gloomy trading statement. The company said Tomb Raider: The Last Revelation and Championship Manager 1999–2000 had performed well in the three months to December 31. However, other titles such as F1 World Grand Prix, Urban Chaos and Abomination recorded weak sales. In addition, Eidos blamed delayed release dates for several titles for adding to the poor quarter. It said this was partly due to too many projects being under development.

The result was that the number of units shipped in the final quarter of the year fell from 6.2m to an estimated 5.9m. Eidos said in its statement: "This implies the results for the financial year ending March 31 2000 will be significantly below those of the previous year." Eidos made pre-tax profits of £37.9m last year on sales of £226.3m.

Charles Cornwall, chief executive, said: "There is no one more humbled by this than I am.

Spare a thought for all those New Economy analysts who seemed so confident that Eidos was cheap at a p/e of 30. After the profits warning the share price sank steadily. The company set itself up as a bid target and there were rumours of a major corporation interested in taking it over – the magic word 'Microsoft'. That didn't materialize, but a French firm turned up, offering their own shares, not cash, as payment. People started writing about the death of the Lara Croft brand, despite a major motion picture with a sequel coming soon.

I wasn't interested anymore; I had got in early, ridden the big price surge and got out. Now it was time to look for new pastures.

Chapter 11

Carphone Warehouse

I used to have a carphone, back in the eighties. I was on the cutting edge of new technology in those days. The thing was the size of a wardrobe. You could walk inside. It didn't have a lid, it had a door. I'm not surprised they called it a carphone – you needed a garage to house the thing.

Alright, I'm exaggerating! It was about the size of a storage heater, and weighed about as much. It was just about as useless as a storage heater, too. You had charge it overnight, and you were lucky if you got ten minutes of use . . . alright, I'm still exaggerating!

My carphone experience was not a happy one, as you can see, which made me a bit more jaded than most when the new, better mobile telephone technology came along.

I found a big potential loser in 2000: Carphone Warehouse, which was about to be floated on the stock market and was aiming at a market capitalization of £1.6–2 billion. That seemed a bit arrogant – as if the £400 million difference between those two estimates wasn't much. As far as I was concerned, the entire company wasn't worth £400 million anyway, but I was no mobile phone expert then, or now.

In the Alanist philosophy, there are many things you don't have to know in order to make a judgement. Carphone Warehouse thought it was worth £1.6–2 billion, but if you took a walk along your local high street in 2000, you could see that everyone was flogging mobile phones, and most people you knew already had one. And if you didn't have a mobile, would you go as far as Carphone Warehouse to get one?

My suspicions were aroused – why were they floating at a time when it looked as if the market for their products was saturated? I looked them up on the *Financial Times* website:

Lex: Carphone Warehouse

(FT.com site, 8 June 2000)

On the sketchy information available on Wednesday, Carphone Warehouse appears rather ambitious in hoping for a market value of GBP1.6bn to GBP2bn ($3bn) when it floats in July. At the top end of that range, the group would be valued at nearly 3 times sales, and 49 times earnings before interest, tax, depreciation, amortisation and exceptionals for the year to March. That looks steep for what is essentially a retailer, even if the products it sells carry the excitement of mobile phones.

No doubt juicy profit forecasts from the syndicate managers' analysts will show the multiples falling sharply this year. But the prospectus, due at the end of the month, will have to be more convincing about CPW's longer term growth prospects. As a retailer it is vulnerable to high costs from a portfolio of short leaseholds, and its staff are paid a sizeable premium. The trading margin of under 6 per cent also reflects losses in Europe. It does have plenty of scope to expand across Europe, with the GBP200m or so of new money it is seeking, and its offer of impartial advice appeals to customers. But it is debatable whether its rivals will allow it to continue its expansion unfettered.

Meanwhile, it is all very well to predict rising mobile phone usage and more frequent replacement sales driven by rapid technology changes, but CPW's profits depend more on maintaining its relationships with the network operators. As these consolidate they will have less incentive to pay CPW for new customers. CPW needs the right product at the right price. So do investors.

Investors would be getting a p/e of about 49, which was a 65% premium to the stock market average at the time. And the stock market average was already double the historic norm.

EBITDA – 'Earnings Before Interest, Taxes, Depreciation and Amortization'. It was a fashionable measure of companies during the 1990s. It measures operating cashflow and is of interest where companies have a lot of fixed assets, such as buildings and machinery, which depreciate (typically manufacturers) or where they have a lot of intangible assets, such as the valuable knowledge in their researchers' heads (such as in high-tech companies). Used intelligently, it can tell accountants and analysts quite a lot about firms with large assets or large debts, but it is not very useful for other types of company.

In my opinion, EBITDA was much abused by the fans and promoters of the telecom companies during the 1990s telecoms boom.

For believers in the new telephony it didn't matter that the market was high. Telecoms were changing the way we live. The telcos were also changing the way they did their accounts, which is something I never feel comfortable about!

I watched the flotation with interest:

Carphone Warehouse IPO will value group at $2.4bn

(FT.com site, 26 June 2000)

Carphone Warehouse, the UK's largest independent mobile phone retailer, on Monday said shares in its initial public offering would be priced between 170p and 220p, valuing the group at about GBP1.6bn ($2.40bn). The global offering of 102.6m new shares and 61.3m existing shares is expected to raise GBP180m for the company. The IPO represents 20 per cent of the group's enlarged shareholding.

Carphone Warehouse said it would use the proceeds of the offer to expand the company through a mixture of acquisitions and organic growth. One third of the cash is to go into developing its telecoms and internet business, partly through acquisitions. A third will be used for expanding the distribution business in Europe and the final third will go towards repaying outstanding debt.

Carphone Warehouse said turnover in the year ended March 25 was GBP679.2m for continuing businesses, an increase of 114.9 per cent on the previous year. Earnings before tax, interest, amortisation, depreciation and exceptional items was GBP33.1m for continuing businesses, an increase of 74.2 per cent.

Following rapid expansion and the recent acquisition of Tandy in the UK, the group has increased its Europe-wide network of shops from 566 to 824 in the past year. It boasts 17 per cent of the UK retail market for phones, and claims to be neck and neck with Dixons Store Group, which jointly owns the nearest rival, Link, together with BT Cellnet.

The company announced recently the launch of Mviva, a European mobile internet portal, in which AOL Europe holds a 15 per cent stake. The Mviva venture, valued at around $700m, may have played a significant role in Carphone Warehouse's valuation, which is higher than previous industry estimates of about GBP800m and comes in spite of recent stock market turbulence.

Questions have been raised, however,about the source of Carphone's tremendous revenue growth and how secure it will be in the future. Much of the money comes from subsidies given by network operators such as Vodafone and Orange to encourage new subscribers.

Yet all four UK operators are looking at ways to regain control of the distribution channel. Cellnet has been investing heavily in existing chains such as Link and DX, while Vodafone and Orange are rolling out their own stores.

Trading in Carphone Warehouse shares is due to begin on July 14.

Credit Suisse First Boston is global co-ordinator for the float, while Morgan Stanley Dean Witter has been appointed as joint lead manager

Hmmm. In paragraph three, the article above tells me that Carphone Warehouse's EBITDA is £33 million. In the previous year it was £19 million. The article doesn't say what the estimated EBITDA for this year is, but I read somewhere else that it was £45 million. That looks like a nice trend of growth, but to me it is screaming that the firm is about to stop growing and that's why they're offloading their shares in the stock market now while the figures still look good.

Naturally the company is talking about future growth. Like all the telcos, it's raving about '3G', the third generation of mobile phone technology that is going to change everything. The analysts are estimating that the firm will have an EBITDA of £135 million in 2005. Personally, I don't believe in five-year plans. I gave them up about the time Stalin did, and for the same reason: they don't work.

I didn't believe that Carphone Warehouse would be earning £135 million in five years' time by flogging mobile phones. In 2000 they were shifting 2.5 million units a year. To earn £135 million, they would have to be selling nearly 10 million units in 2005. No wonder the firm was diversifying. But I didn't like the look of what they were diversifying into: a mobile internet portal called Mviva, valued at $700million, nearly half the company's market capitalization.

I did some quick sums. Suppose they achieved their estimated EBITDA this year of £45 million. Knock off, say, 20% for exceptional items, take off the tax, and you're looking at £25 million for earnings. This was a single product retailer in a soon-to-be saturated market with little prospect of earnings growth. What's worse, all its main competitors were also its main suppliers.

This firm didn't pay a dividend and its p/e was to be 49 when it floated. Water companies currently had a p/e of under 9, and were paying a 6% dividend. So would Carphone Warehouse eventually drop to a p/e of 9? I couldn't see that happening in the current market. Suppose they dropped to a p/e of 18? That would make their share price 65p, which is roughly what I thought the company was worth.

I felt that the market wouldn't be long in driving it down to that level. I decided to sell it short and wait for as long as it took.

The issue went well for Carphone Warehouse. The share price opened on a Friday at 225p, which put it at a premium. On the following Monday, though, it had dropped to 190p. I waited. By October the price was down to 150p. I decided to take some profits by closing out some of my CFDs because the interim results were due in November, and they might put the share price up. I kept the rest of the CFDs for the longer term.

Carphone Warehouse maiden results show strong growth

(FT.com site, 6 November 2000)

Carphone Warehouse, the UK's largest independent mobile phone retailer, on Monday reported nearly 1.5m new connections in the past six months, a rise of 74 per cent from the same period one year earlier. The growth came from subscriptions, where customers enter into airtime contracts, and pre-pay sales.

Reporting their first results since flotation, Carphone said turnover for the half year to September 23 rose 62 per cent to GBP447.9m from GBP277.3m. Pre-tax profit was GBP17.4m (GBP6.6m), which included an exceptional gain of GBP16.5m from the investment by AOL Europe in Mviva. AOL owns a 15 per cent stake in the European mobile internet portal. Mviva now has more than 50,000 subscribers, up from 30,000 at the end of September.

Overall gross operating margins were down from 25.5 per

cent to 24.7 per cent reflecting the growth of the lower margin wholesale business.

Carphone operates 1009 stores in 14 markets against 608 stores in nine markets last year. It spent GBP68m on new stores, six acquisitions and improvements to its operating systems.

Carphone shares closed up 6p at 198p.

It all sounded like good news for the company. But the thing about exceptional gains is that now you see them, now you don't. The exceptional gain of £16.5 million from Mviva looked rather convenient. If you subtracted £16.5 million from the pretax profit of £17.4 million, you were left with a £900,000 profit from the main mobile phone business, which is pathetically low for a firm of that size. I stayed short.

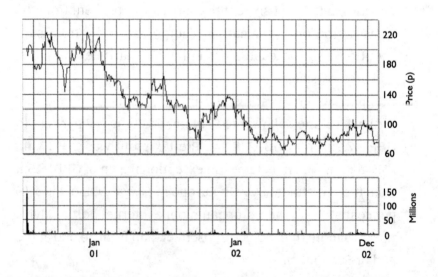

Figure 11.1 Carphone Warehouse 2000–2003

From Figure 11.1 you can see what happened to the share price during 2002 and 2003. It was truly horrible, if you happened to be an investor. As a short seller, I made a lot of money – it was one of those big losers that worked out very well indeed.

Chapter 12

Telewest Communications

Telewest Communications was a company that offered consumers cable TV. I took against it quite early on. Satellite TV was already available, and the price of the satellite dishes was coming down, so I reckoned cable systems were going to lose out.

The trouble with cable TV is that you have to dig up all the pavements to lay cable. The cost is horrendous – all that earth moving, all that labour and disruption. It wasn't exactly an elegant solution to the problem of getting all the new TV channels to every home in Britain.

Telewest always seemed to have a new story about some new bit of technology that was going to get them out of their mess. One minute it was pay-TV and it was going to be providing cheap telephone calls through their cables. Then it was video-on-demand; next, the internet; next, digital; next, broadband.

Billions and billions of pounds were poured into the Telewest hole. And that's what I didn't understand. The hole kept getting deeper, but the share price kept on rising.

In 1998 I gave them another year before the price collapsed. I had rented a flat in Bristol, where the company was based, and wanted to get Sky TV. Satellite dishes weren't allowed in my building, so I had to go to Telewest. It was like stepping back in time. It reminded me of British Telecom in the days when it was a nationalized monster. All I wanted was a cable TV connection. I phoned and phoned and phoned. When I occasionally got through, they would tell me that I could have the connection, but I had to wait.

The last straw was when they offered me a free phone and wanted me to cancel my British Telecom account. Not likely! Everything about them told me they weren't long for this world. Then, after a while I started to wonder if it was just me. I asked other customers. Nobody had a good word to say about them. So why was the share price rising?

Telewest attacks BSkyB price rise

(*Financial Times*, 22 January 1998)

Telewest Communications, the UK's second biggest cable company, yesterday blamed price increases by BSkyB, its main supplier of television programmes, for a rise in the number of customers failing to renew their subscriptions last year.

The so-called churn rate was most marked in the fourth quarter when it rose from 27.1 to 35 per cent among the group's television customers. In the 12 months to the end of December, the rate increased from 33.4 to 34 per cent. Charles Burdick, finance director, blamed the latest BSkyB price rise for the lack of customer interest: 'This is the customers saying to Sky, "We have had enough".' He added that the increase had encouraged Telewest's involvement in the cable consortium, which will launch its own pay-per-view film channel shortly.

The company is also introducing a low-cost television and telephone package next month and is in talks with Flextech to supply programmes for a separate channel, further reducing its reliance on BSkyB.

Mr Burdick said he believed the Flextech deal would force BSkyB to 'unbundle' the broadcaster's programme package and allow subscribers to choose the channels they required. This would lead to a rise in the number of homes taking the service and a churn reduction.

He pointed to Telewest's trial of the low-cost package in Scotland – soon to be offered nationwide – which resulted in penetration rates of 50 per cent and churn of below 20 per cent.

'If we get these kind of figures from the rest of our franchises, our position will be transformed,' said Mr Burdick.

BSkyB has resisted unbundling because of the risk of lower revenues.

Can you make sense of that? I bet you that BSkyB couldn't. They must have been too busy laughing all the way to the bank. I would have loved to have been a fly on the wall at the consortium meetings – can you imagine what the guys from Sky might have been saying when Telewest were out of earshot? How did these people expect to make money when they were relying on Sky for their programming, and Sky were pushing satellites?

I would have liked to have gone short, but with all that money pouring in I had to wait while the losses piled up. In 1998 they lost £300 million. In 1999 they lost £500 million. The share price kept rising. By March 2000 the share price was in orbit at 563p (see Figure 12.1) – that meant the market was valuing Telewest at £12.9 billion.

Figure 12.1 Telewest Communications 1996–2002

In my book you have to accept it when the flow is going against you. The market wasn't ready to turn on Telewest. I thought it over: suppose, hypothetically, I had £12 billion and I could either keep it on risk-free deposit at 6% or I could buy 100% of Telewest. What sort of potential return would I need to take the risk? 12%? 18%? Let's say 18% – that would give me an extra 12%, say 8% net, in return for risking my capital. On the other hand, if I put my £12 billion in the building society at 6% I would be getting £14 million a week. Telewest was currently losing about £12 million a week.

And how long could they go losing that kind of money – about half a billion pounds a year? Something had to give. I made my decision and went short on Telewest.

It took a while for things to change but they did eventually:

Downgrade hits Telewest

(*Financial Times*, 22 July 2000)

Grassroots research by a City analyst yesterday sparked selling of Telewest Communications, the cable operator, after it became known that a components shortage would delay the roll-out of Telewest's digital television decoders. The shares fell 9 per cent to end the day at 235p.

Stephen Scruton, an analyst at HSBC, downgraded the cable operator to "sell" after Telewest's customer services told him that the roll-out of the decoders had been suspended.

"After being put on hold for 10 minutes and being thrown out of the line, I waited for another 10 minutes only to be told that I would have to wait for three to four months to get a box," he said.

Telewest, meanwhile, denied the extent of the wait. Instead, it said the components shortage "is causing a slight touch on our brakes."

"In common with the rest of the cable industry, Telewest is experiencing short-term problems accessing sufficient set-top boxes to cope with demand from customers for our digital services."

Pace Micro Technology, which is Telewest's exclusive supplier of decoders, warned earlier in the month that it anticipated the supply to remain tight.

People close to the company maintained that the delay would not have a "material impact on its earnings". Analysts generally agreed but said the delay would worsen sentiment.

In 1999, Telewest's pre-tax loss widened from £313.6m to $529.9m on sales of £792.5m

"A slight touch on our brakes," said Telewest. Don't you just love it? As if it would all have been plain sailing except for a minor delay in getting the decoders. Look at what happened to the price in 2002 (Figure 12.1) – I shed no tears for them.

Chapter 13

Safeway

If you live out in the countryside as I do, shopping is a major chore. The shops are all miles away, and when you get there finding a parking space is a nightmare. In Minehead, my nearest town, the car park is a long walk from the shops so you're liable to get soaked in a rainstorm as an added bonus.

Minehead is one of those dreary West Country towns that is completely user-unfriendly. Arthur C. Clarke, the science fiction writer, was born there, which is perhaps why he lives in Sri Lanka now – Minehead's about as different as you can get from a tropical paradise. There's a Tesco supermarket, which is where I used to do my shopping, more because I could park there than because of what it sold. I went in once at midnight and it was like *The Night of the Living Dead*. Even the shelves were empty and there was a weird, pale blue light, like something out of the *X Files*. I only wanted some cigarettes, but there were a few shuffling figures, doing their weekly shopping in the freezer section.

Shopping at Minehead was beginning to depress me. There had to be another way. Occasionally we would pop down to Penzance in Cornwall for a break. Penzance has a big Safeway supermarket and we would always load up there. I don't know why, but everything seemed bigger and better at Safeway. It had wider aisles, wider smiles and a wider choice. The prices were good, too.

I started becoming a Safeway fanatic. I couldn't stay away from it while we were in Penzance and kept going back every day. Then I started to check out other Safeway stores on my travels. I made a list of which supermarket outlets I liked best. Everywhere I went, Safeway was at the top, Tesco was in between and Sainsbury's was at the bottom. I didn't know exactly what I was looking for, but I knew what I liked – Safeway. Tesco was too downmarket, and Sainsbury's always seemed drab.

In the summer of 1999 food retailers were out of favour in the stock market. Technology was the obsession and the supermarkets were looking very 'old economy'. I was sure that the technology bubble was going to burst and investors would 'fly to safety' in more traditional businesses, like food retailers. Safeway was also getting a new chief executive, Carlos Criado-Perez, who had come from WalMart, the American retailing giant. From what I have seen, WalMart people know what they are doing, so this was promising news. In fact, WalMart had wanted to take over Safeway, which was even more promising.

I kept following the story:

Lex: Safeway
(*Financial Times*, 24 November 2000)
They call it the Carlos effect. Few would have believed a year ago that Safeway, struggling number four in UK food retailing, could have been revitalised as it has by chief executive Carlos Criado-Perez. But believing that the recovery can be sustained means putting an awful lot of faith in the retailing wizardry of the former Wal-Mart executive.

Phase one – getting more shoppers into Safeway's aisles – has been a success. Eschewing Wal-Mart-style everyday low pricing in favour of "high-low" pricing, or aggressive promotions on 50 key products a week, has increased the number of customer transactions by 10 per cent. Like-for-like sales grew 5 per cent in the first half, with gross margins also up.

Phase two – getting shoppers to pile more into their trolleys – is tricky. Part of Mr Criado-Perez's strategy is expanding some superstores into scaled-down, continental European-style hypermarkets, adding homewares, DIY and entertainment goods. Getting that right in the UK is notoriously difficult. It also looks a bit like an admission that, having pledged to do so, Mr Criado-Perez no longer believes he can get Safeway's sales densities up to the level of Tesco and Sainsbury, and is instead resorting to the old Safeway strategy: spend lots of money on increasing floorspace.

But, with tangible proof that a recovery is under way, Safeway's shares do not deserve their discount to Sainsbury. And if the bounceback continues and Safeway bulks up its stores, the chances of an Asda takeover in a year or two – Competition Commission permitting – can only increase

Carlos Criado-Perez was doing his job the way I had hoped he would. By the following spring he'd produced some real results. The share price had soared to triple its low in March 2000 (see Figure 13.1).

Safeway claims turnaround is complete

(*Financial Times*, 16 May 2001)
Safeway, the UK's fourth-largest grocer, on Wednesday gave a convincing demonstration that it had recovered from past woes as it unveiled rising annual sales and profits.

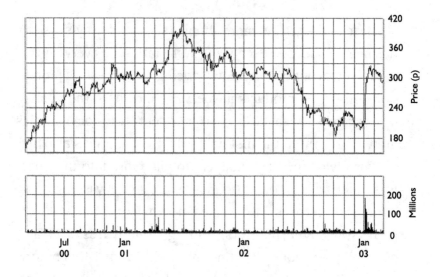

Figure 13.1 Safeway 2000–2003

The group declared its turnaround was complete and said it could now concentrate on store refurbishments and improving its food ranges and customer service.

Like-for-like sales in the 52 weeks to March 31 were 5.2 per cent higher, while pre-tax profits rose more than 33 per cent to GBP314.5m ($448m), in line with expectations of GBP295m–GBP320m. Total sales were GBP8.9bn compared with GBP8.3bn in the same period one year earlier

Not long after the turnaround was announced, the share price started to slide. It had been a classic case of "Buy on the expectation, sell on the news", but it had been good while it lasted.

Then things got really interesting. A year later, in mid-2002, I was experiencing *déjà vu*. Safeway's share price was back where it started and I happened to be back in Penzance. I stopped at Safeway to load up on shopping and the whole story came back to me. As I was filling my trolley I was thinking, why not really go long on Safeway? The lower the share price went, the more likely it was that another food giant would try to take the company over. I knew that WalMart was interested and would make a bid immediately if they were given a green light by the regulators. There had to be other companies who would be interested.

Meanwhile Safeway was trading at £2 a share, which was a lovely low p/e of 8. Compare that with Tesco, which was on a p/e of 18. Why would you buy Tesco in preference to Safeway? Why hold Tesco in preference to Safeway? Why shop in Tesco in preference to Safeway?

Safeway was going to be a big winner, so I filled my boots with CFDs and waited.

Safeway: retailer is key to consolidation

(*Financial Times*, 29 October 2002)

Do not expect Safeway to go quietly – or quickly. Britain's fourth-biggest supermarket chain may be caught in the centre of a whirlwind of takeover rumours, but the group is the key strategic piece in the jigsaw of food retailing consolidation in the UK.

The latest rumours to engulf Safeway concern a break-up bid by venture capitalists and bankers. In the background are the long-term whispers that Asda – in the shape of its US parent Wal-Mart – is planning a bid. To add spice to that morsel is the belief that Wal-Mart has held talks with JSainsbury about the possibility of a joint bid.

So what is the attraction of Safeway? Generally regarded as the weakest of the top five players, the group has the worst store portfolio and the least powerful brand. All the recent news on trading shows it is underperforming its rivals in spite of the intensive surgery carried out by Carlos Criado Perez, the former Wal-Mart executive.

But the group is strong in southern England – where both Asda and Morrison are weak – and in Scotland – where Sainsbury would love to grow. It also owns the freehold to about 75 per cent of its stores and, in spite of the sales underperformance, is still growing and retains a strong balance sheet.

There is also no doubt that Mr Criado Perez has done amazingly well considering the task he was handed when he joined Safeway three years ago. The business is substantially better than before his arrival. And the flamboyant retailer has more up his sleeve.

The key risk for any bidder is the Competition Commission. Its last study of the supermarket sector made great play of the need to retain as many different facias as possible and stressed the need to avoid local as well as national monopolies.

Financial bidders could have little confidence of whom they could sell the assets on to if they bid. A trade buyer or buyers would face the same problem – but have the added attraction of being able to bid more because of the substantial synergies such a deal would offer.

The share price would seem to suggest that a bid remains remote. Closing yesterday at 221p, the shares may have risen almost 5 per cent on the rumours, but they remain well below the level of any likely bid. If the group was taken out at the same multiple that Asda was, that would give a price of more than 500p a share. That may be unrealistic, but Safeway shareholders are likely to want at least 300p.

So, rumours of bids are in the air but the *FT* thinks chances of one materializing are remote – reading between the lines, I felt confident that one would emerge, especially when I read the following article a couple of days later:

Safeway's web

(*Financial Times*, 1 November 2002)

Carlos Criado-Perez is playing the innocent foreigner abroad. Passionately defending the supermarket group he leads, he insists that Safeway has a long future ahead as an independent.

No way does he want to sell out to evil, bigger competitors such as Wal-Mart – for which, incidentally, he used to work. "I am not a wheeler-dealer," the charismatic grocer tells Observer. "I am a foreigner here and I don't have the contacts to be like that."

Fear not, Carlos. Your chairman David Webster has spent 25 years at Safeway and knows everyone you could ever need to know.

Why takeovers can be good for shareholders

If you own shares in a company that becomes an acquisition target, the chances are that the share price will rise. The reason for this is that the acquiring firm often has to pay a premium over the market value of the shares in order to buy the company. Strict stock market rules on takeover announcements force bidders to announce quite early in the process, to keep it fair. Once a preliminary announcement has been made, the share price is likely to rise. A bid may fail for many reasons, so it may be better to sell while the bidding is going on and the share price is up than to wait for the final settlement and find that the bid – and the share price – collapses.

Over the years, numerous academic studies of corporate mergers and acquisitions (M&A) have produced quite alarming evidence that the acquiring firm – the 'predator' – frequently gets a bad bargain. The price paid is often too high, and the promised benefits, such as the sharing of research and development costs, fail to materialize. This is bad news for the shareholders of the acquiring company, because it means that the purchase may ultimately reduce the value of their shares.

So why are M&A so popular when there is the money around to fund them? The answer lies in the natural tension that exists between the owners and managers of a company – that is, the shareholders and the top executives. Top executives may obtain all kinds of benefits to their careers, status and personal wealth by going along with a merger that they know, in their heart of hearts, may not be in the best long term interests of the company or its shareholders.

Of course, shareholders can be short-termist too. Buying shares in firms that are potential acquisition targets is a great way to speculate, and often quite low risk if you only pick large firms. If your guess is right, you can be richly rewarded.

Evidently the FT's crystal ball was in good shape. The supermarket chain Morrison soon made a bid and after Christmas it looked as if we might be in for that shareholder's bonanza, a bidding war:

Safeway shares rise on talk of counter bids

(*Financial Times*, 9 January 2003)

Shares in Safeway rose sharply on Friday as speculation increased of a counter offer for the UK supermarket chain in the wake of Wm Morrison's agreed £2.65bn ($4.26bn) paper bid.

Rivals J Sainsbury and Wal-Mart, the US owner of Asda, refused to rule out the possibility of launching a cash bid, either together or separately.

The two sides – who held talks about a possible joint approach last year – are expected to resume negotiations over the weekend, or early next week. People close to both sides said if they decided to move they could do so quickly – with one saying that a bid could come as early as next week.

Analysts said any bid by the duo would have to be in the region of 350p to 400p

That price rise was good enough for me – I closed out my position with a healthy profit.

Chapter 14

New Look

Living out in a remote part of Exmoor, we felt a bit cut off from the latest trends. How excited we were when we set off on the thirty mile drive to our nearest major shopping centre, Taunton.

When we got there, I took my teenage daughter into a clothes shop called New Look. It was packed with customers having a feeding frenzy. I couldn't see why – the goods all looked pretty tatty to me, but I don't know anything about fashion. My daughter tried on half the shop, and then bought the other half. I decided to do a bit of informal research.

"Is it always like this?" I asked the assistant. "It has been, recently", she said.

"Why?"

She gave me a look as if I'd just arrived from Mars. "Well, it's better, innit?"

After New Look, we went to Starbucks to have a triple latte. "So what's with New Look?" I asked my daughter, who now seemed to own most of their stock.

"Dad!"

"Dad what?"

"It's mega, that's what."

"Mega, as in?"

"Dad, if I've got to explain it, you're not going to get it." She gave me a look that was even more pitying than the one the shop assistant had given me. She was quite right, I didn't get it – but I did understand that teenage girls got it, whatever it was.

I went home to research New Look. If their customers loved the place, maybe the company was a buy. But the shop was in Taunton, which is hardly the fashion centre of the universe, so I wasn't going to get too carried away.

New Look had a p/e of 4. Now, I like low p/es, but a p/e of 4 looks like a terminal illness. I had noticed it before because it was so low and had just assumed that it was about to go out of business. I hadn't even known that there was a New Look outlet in Taunton.

It turned out that New Look's senior management had all left rather suddenly, taking big golden parachutes with them. It had started as a single shop in Weymouth, and after three decades there were 300 shops and a profit, in 94, of over £10 million. The firm had tried to float in 1994, but the City had given them the cold shoulder.

In 1997 they went back to the City with 450 shops and profits of £32 million. The City listened this time. New Look floated in June 1998 at 165p, which capitalized the business at £330 million. That was a nice round number: 33 years of work to create an asset worth £330 million. Profits for the year ending March 1999 were forecast to rise to over £40 million.

The forecast had been right: the actual figure was £41 million. After a shaky start the share price started to go up too. It took some time, partly because the market crashed in the autumn of 1998 when Russia defaulted on its bonds and Long Term Capital Management collapsed. Long Term Capital Management, you may remember, was a team of Nobel Prize-winning geniuses in the US who had worked out a foolproof system for beating the markets. The markets beat them, and they owed so much they nearly brought the whole thing down.

New Look went as low as 120p during the autumn of 1998 but by March of 1999 the market had recovered, and New Look's price was back where it had started. By the time they announced their results in June the price was hitting 240p.

I started researching them in April 2001, when the stock market was down by 15% and New Look had sunk to 65p. It was a bit depressing. Everything that could have gone wrong had done so. They had lost their Chief Executive, they had had to appoint a new Finance Director, and issued two profit warnings blaming the fuel crisis for their problems when half their customers weren't old enough to have a driving licence, let alone own a car.

But they had still made a profit of £47 million and the forecast for the year just ended was £31 million. Okay, so the profit was down, but not appallingly so. At a share price of 65p the market was valuing New Look at only £120 million. That was ridiculous – £120 million was what they took in three months' worth of sales in their 500 shops. If they were going to start having feeding frenzies like the one I had just seen in Taunton, it would take less than three months to turn over £120 million.

This company was cheap. I would never have realized this by just looking at my computer screen. Thanks to my daughter, I had learned that New Look was very much alive. And the clincher was what the sales assistant had said about the shop: "Well, it's better, innit?" She meant that New Look had somehow made itself more attractive to its customers. Maybe the stock market didn't know this yet.

The question now was, what was this nugget of information worth? Should I go long on New Look now, or should I wait? In a few weeks' time the company would publish its annual results and, most importantly, the trading statement, which would give some idea of the future.

When that was published everyone would know that New Look wasn't such a dog after all. I decided to go long on New Look right away – just as soon as I had checked out their outlets in Bristol to make sure that Taunton hadn't been a one-off. It was Saturday and I was due in Bristol on Tuesday. I decided to take out a few CFDs on Monday, and if Bristol confirmed my opinion I would buy more.

The sector p/e was 16. New Look's p/e was 4. I felt that the share price had to at least double once the good news got out. I rang my friend Suzi in Brighton and asked her to go and look at the New Look there. I decided that if Bristol and Brighton were good, I would put £120,000 at risk.

The New Look shops in Brighton and Bristol were all that I'd hoped they would be, so I went ahead. I didn't have long to wait for a very sweet profit indeed:

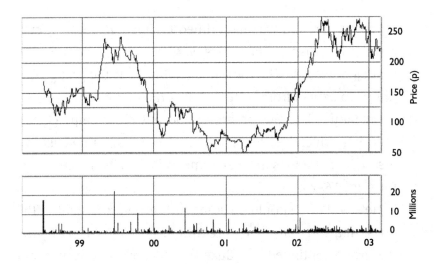

Figure 14.1 New Look share price 1999–2002

Better times for New Look

(Alison Smith, *Financial Times*, 29 May2002)

New Look put the troubles of the past firmly behind it yesterday, as it reported record sales and pre-tax profits for the year to March 30.

But Stephen Sunnucks, chief executive of the discount fashion retailer, expressed caution about the outlook, warning that market conditions could get tougher.

"We are very confident about our strategy, but we're planning to keep stock and costs very tight," he said." Who knows what the coming months will bring in terms of interest rates, consumer spending and confidence."

The performance contrasted markedly with the group's previous experience: the last set of full-year results was proceeded by two profit warnings, a boardroom shake-up and a share price that fell as low as 50p.

The turnaround was underlined by improvements in current trading: like-for-like sales were up 16.3 per cent for the first eight weeks of the new financial year, as the group continued to benefit from better product ranges and distribution.

Mr Sunnocks said the group had put more emphasis on tailoring, which had proved important in attracting customers in their twenties, and had done well from its Inspire range for sizes 16–24.

He said there should be some further improvement in the gross margin – up 4.1 percentage points last year – as the group continued to reduce the level of mark-downs, but most of this would come in the first half.

Group sales rose from £469.8m to £585.4m for the 53 week period, while pre-tax profit more than doubled to £62.3m.

A final dividend of 4.8p (4p) makes a total of 7p (6.1p), payable from earnings of 19.8p (10.4).

The shares rose 3p to close at 268p.

So what is the message of this book?

First, go with what *you* know. Forget what you read or are told and open your eyes to what you are experiencing in your daily life as a consumer. Do this and you will be your own best investment advisor. *Shopping for Profit* as we call it.

Second, CFDs and spread-betting techniques are the tools that enable you to profit from your observations.

This is not their only use, however. In our next book we will reveal the unique CFD/spread-betting trading techniques we have used to trade millions of pounds a day with minimum risk and maximum returns.

In the meantime for further information we can be contacted as follows:

> www.thestreetwiseinvestor.com
> knowhow@thestreetwiseinvestor.com

> The Streetwise Investor
> Suite 106
> 14 Clifton Down Road
> Bristol BS8 4BF

All readers expressing interest in the next book will receive details of our zero-risk two-way win–win trading strategy.

Index

Alan Moore enjoyed a highly successful career in the financial services industry. In 1980 he founded what was rapidly to become one of the largest firms of independent investment advisors in the country. In 1987, backed by the recently retired chairman of ICI (Sir John Harvey-Jones), he became the Chief Executive of Burns-Anderson PLC. Retiring at the age of 40 since then he has been an active private investor, studied theology at Oxford, written a regular column for the Guardian and currently acts as a consultant within the gaming industry.

James Moore is currently reading Computer Science at Downing College, Cambridge. He is the co-author of the highly acclaimed book *Professional PHP Programming*.

Capstone Publishing (A Wiley company)
John Wiley & Sons Ltd
The Atrium
Southern Gate
Chichester
West Sussex
PO19 8SQ

Tel: +44 (0) 1243 779 777
Fax: +44 (0) 1243 770 638

Info@wiley-capstone.co.uk
www.wileyeurope.com

Cover design by Cylinder
Cover image ©ImageState/Alamy